Andi Stix & Frank Hrbek

Teachers as Classroom Coaches

How to Motivate Students Across the Content Areas

Association for Supervision and Curriculum Development
Alexandria, Virginia USA

Association for Supervision and Curriculum Development
1703 N. Beauregard St. • Alexandria, VA 22311-1714 USA
Phone: 800-933-2723 or 703-578-9600 • Fax: 703-575-5400
Web site: www.ascd.org • E-mail: member@ascd.org
Author guidelines: www.ascd.org/write

Gene R. Carter, *Executive Director;* Nancy Modrak, *Director of Publishing;* Julie Houtz, *Director of Book Editing & Production;* Ernesto Yermoli, *Project Manager;* Greer Beeken, *Graphic Designer;* Circle Graphics, *Typesetter;* Dina Murray Seamon, *Production Specialist/Team Lead*

PAPERBACK ISBN-13: 978-1-4166-0411-2   ASCD product #106031   s10/06
Also available as an e-book through ebrary, netLibrary, and many online booksellers (see Books in Print for the ISBNs).

Quantity discounts for the paperback edition only: 10–49 copies, 10%; 50+ copies, 15%; for 1,000 or more copies, call 800-933-2723, ext. 5634, or 703-575-5634. For desk copies: member@ascd.org.

Library of Congress Cataloging-in-Publication Data

Stix, Andi.
   Teachers as classroom coaches: how to motivate students across the content areas / Andi Stix & Frank Hrbek.
       p. cm.
   Includes bibliographical references and index.
   ISBN-13: 978-1-4166-0411-2 (pbk. : alk. paper)
   ISBN-10: 1-4166-0411-1 (pbk. : alk. paper) 1. Motivation in education. 2. Effective teaching. I. Hrbek, Frank, 1937- II. Title.

   LB1065.S832 2006
   370.15'4—dc22

                                                                              2006019742

_____

14 13 12 11 10 09 08 07 06   1 2 3 4 5 6 7 8 9 10 11 12

For our families,

who gave love and nurturing understanding

while the book was being written

and unstinting support as we matured as educators,

and especially for our children,

who have chosen to follow in our footsteps.

Teachers as
Classroom Coaches

How to Motivate Students Across the Content Areas

Acknowledgments

We must acknowledge and give thanks to the many people who helped bring our endeavors to a successful conclusion. So many gave willingly of their time and effort to test our ideas and review the manuscript: Joyce Kent, head of the Science Department at New Rochelle High School, New Rochelle, New York; Judi Sternberg and Joanne Sapper McKinsley, retired heads of Gifted and Talented Services in Greenburg, New York, and Amarillo, Texas, respectively; Abraham Tannenbaum, professor emeritus at Columbia University; Joseph Postiglione, Sue Nodine, and Carmine Leo at iPEC Coaching; Michael Pastena at Advisors' Education Group; and Michael Yazurlo, superintendent of the Tuckahoe Public School System, Tuckahoe, New York. A special thank you to Suzanne Staszak-Silva for undertaking the initial task of editing and fine-tuning the pages we sent her way. Most importantly, we were blessed with two editors at ASCD, Carolyn Pool and Ernesto Yermoli, who gave us encouragement when it was most needed and the advice to make our vision a reality.

Special thanks are extended to the principals, administrators, and teachers of two New York City schools: Lower East Side Preparatory High School (in lower Manhattan) and Life Sciences Secondary School (on 96th Street between 1st and 2nd Avenues). The former has a predominantly Asian American population, and the latter is majority African American and Latino. Principals Martha Polin and Genevieve Stanislaus allowed us to work with their teaching staffs and introduce coaching strategies into their educational environments. In both schools, the Social Studies departments served as our principal test sites. Our experiences at both locations were gratifying and rewarding, especially the professional development sessions with the faculties and the training sessions with individual staff members. Both departments have shown a continual positive improvement that is most evident in higher test scores and a complementary lowering of behavioral conflicts within the classroom.

At Life Sciences Secondary School, we were given the opportunity to train students who were selected by their teachers and guidance counselors for their excellent social skills. For two months, meeting at 8:00 a.m., youngsters traveled from the far reaches of the New York City area to be trained in "Leadership Coaching." Students found that their listening skills were vastly improved, and their ability to foster their peers' talents effectively became more proficient. Working with 16- and 17-year-olds in this fashion was exhilarating!

—Andi Stix and Frank Hrbek

Introduction

The golfer is picture perfect: arms back, shoulders straight, head down. The concentration is intense. The whack of the club is like the crack of a whip, and the follow-through is a wonder of precision as the ball shoots endlessly down the fairway.

Tiger Woods has wowed them again.

As the golfer takes his first confident strides toward his second shot, somewhere, unnoticed among the onlookers, his coach smiles with satisfaction. His pupil has mastered his lessons.

Sports coaches have always pushed their star athletes and franchise players to live up to their potential and maximize their performance. They achieve superb results by building a trusting relationship and by creating an environment in which their pupils' stress levels decrease as their success ratios spiral upward. Coaches inspire by actively guiding their pupils to take risks and face challenges.

Why does the coaching system work so well in sports? The coaches themselves are an important factor, of course, but most significant is the fact that the athletes are thrust rapidly into real-life experiences. The efforts of coaches, such as encouraging continuous practice or researching the opposition's techniques, are all focused on furthering the players' endeavors and sharpening their skills. These are athletes who perform for their peers and fans. Coaches help players use their time according to a clearly defined purpose and with a specific goal in mind.

Coaching is widely known in the business world, as well. It is not uncommon today for CEOs, high level administrators, and managers to have personal executive or life coaches.

During a training session at the Institute for Professional Empowerment Coaching (iPEC), a firm known for preparing executive and life coaches, professional coach Deborah Van de Grift stated that an investment in coaching offers a fabulous return in the following areas:

Environment
- Improves morale
- Increases a shared vision and mission
- Helps create a warmer cultural environment

Communication
- Enhances honesty
- Improves communication skills
- Develops better listening skills
- Increases the ability to resolve conflicts

Productivity
- Encourages better organization
- Improves team performance
- Increases the ability to achieve corporate and cooperative goals
- Promotes continuous innovation and enhances profitability

Human Resources
- Helps decrease employee tardiness and absenteeism
- Improves client attendance
- Increases employee retention
- Reduces the need for recruitment dollars
- Allows for better hiring decisions

How can we take the models of sports and corporate coaching and apply them to education? We can only hope that our efforts, which are a modification of life and corporate coaching approaches, will bring a semblance of change and innovation to the educational sector. Still, we know that the strategies and activities proposed in this book work because we have tested them ourselves over 30 years of teaching in public schools. Our approach emphasizes bringing out the talents of our students so that they can perform academic content in front of their peers, much as athletes perform in front of spectators and teammates. When the content comes alive in this way, students become engaged and motivated.

Educational Utopia

Just imagine a school where there is a feeling of warmth upon entering; where administrators, teachers, and students feel a sense of ownership in a shared vision and mission. The climate is inviting and friendly, and people work cooperatively. You look at some of the bulletin boards and notice that teachers work between as well as across grade levels, imaginatively breaking down the walls between the classrooms. The administration, teachers, and students are so supported in this trusting environment that you can *feel* the engaging morale and the spirited, dynamic culture.

As you walk through the hallways, you notice that the communication among teachers is open and honest, and that they support the ever-growing process of a viable school that is forever changing in needs and desires. Most importantly, you hear dialogues among students and between teachers and students; they listen to each other in a distinctive way that lets the speaker know that what is being said is valued.

Peeking into classrooms, you see teachers and students designing new projects on a continuous basis because risk-taking is applauded. Rough initial results become as refined as a polished diamond. Behavioral problems are rare, due partly to a coaching program that is extended to working parents at PTA meetings. The classrooms are hives of activity, with students preparing for discussion exercises in which all voices are heard and accountable. Students work well together in their groups, meshing ideas to reach a common goal; they are encouraged to bring charts, graphs, diagrams, and pictures to enhance their performance, and they are made to feel as though they have ownership of their learning. Their discussions, which include multiple perspectives, encourage tolerance. By accepting other viewpoints, students solve problems and conflicts through negotiation and compromise. Due to student motivation and engagement, test scores are high.

On returning to the main office, you notice that over 95 percent of the faculty's time cards are in, and that no one was listed as tardy. When you ask the principal about the personnel turnover rate, the response is a broad smile and the following retort: "Who would ever want to transfer from a school as cooperative and nurturing as this one?"

Does it all sound like an educational utopia? Maybe, but if coaching can have such positive effects in the corporate world, why couldn't it do the same in our schools? As Bobby Kennedy used to say, "Some men see things as they are and ask, 'Why?' I dream things that never were and ask, 'Why not?'"

About This Book

In this book, we offer a new coaching methodology that helps teachers encourage students to "talk content" in a meaningful way. The procedures and strategies presented engage students in project-based learning, during which they are challenged to actively participate in the workshop model of inquiry. Most importantly, this book offers a means of increasing literacy by having students talk and write about content in preparation for a forum, debate, simulation, or presentation.

Section 1: Creating the Coaching Environment

The book is presented in two major sections. In Section 1, we examine what it means to use coaching techniques in the classroom, how to coach students to maximize their performance, how to help students build confidence in taking risks, and how to develop a trusting environment where stress levels decrease as students gain the confidence to attain success. We also offer effective ways to group students so that they can work more productively together, such as by establishing mutual expectations and using contextual listening to create an egalitarian environment that encourages active research and a higher level of learning.

In Section 1, you will also find techniques for helping students with problem solving and for coaching students in the inquiry method of research, which helps students uncover details and multiple perspectives and compels them to make their own critical judgments. The techniques discussed facilitate learning, offer constant encouragement, and help students focus on what is gained by uncovering content. Specific, content-based questions promote extensive in-depth study and offer higher-level thinking while challenging basic assumptions and obsolete notions. Coaching combined with contextual listening skills encourages creative thinking, problem solving, and the lively exchange of ideas. The questioning methods used in coaching also help to reveal what prevents students from performing at a higher level.

Research has shown that students recall higher percentages of the information they study when they teach each other and are active in their own learning (Semb & Ellis, 1994). Their potential to reach the highest standards is raised when the teacher takes on the role of coach to prepare the class for simulations or project-based assignments. As explored in this book, coaching goes beyond being a simple technique; it is also a nurturing attitude that engenders students' best performances.

Students feel respected and important when they are involved in a flexible atmosphere that supports individual, small-group, and whole-group strategies and activities. Faced with a variety of learning formats, students will eagerly attend class because they know that something different is bound to happen. It is our goal to offer teachers a buffet of choice—that is, to allow them to match the content to the best teaching strategy for a vibrant and dynamic learning environment.

Section 2: Classroom Strategies

In Section 2 of the book, we offer detailed explanations of strategies to help students read, write, talk, and listen to meaningful content. Our favorite comment by a student who participated in one of our coaching programs was, "I have a friend who always cuts school, but he never cuts Social Studies. That's the one class he likes, where he has fun. He likes the activities, and he always says he comes away having learned something."

For the educator, the first goal is to create a realistic setting where students present before their peers and assess both themselves and others. Within this setting, the second goal is to infuse literacy across the content areas and "talk content." Educators must give students the tools and wherewithal to make the content come alive. The third goal is to use the strategies described in this book to help the students work together to prepare for an experience, discussion, debate, or simulation.

The coaching methods outlined in Section 2 invite teachers to create a participatory environment for students. We encourage an activity- or project-based classroom where learning is hands-on and inquiry skills are an essential tool. Students are challenged to dig deeper into the content because they are required to use the information publicly and present their work to their peers rather than simply memorize the information for an exam.

Students are motivated by participating in interdisciplinary activities. Encouraging students to push beyond the boundaries of their own expectations by taking risks is intrinsic to our philosophy of coaching. Experience-centered lessons help students to reach their potential by emphasizing content, process, and production, and by having the students use as many modes of learning and assessment as necessary to engage their talents.

Relating content to students' own lives is also integral to our philosophy. Experience-based learning can help students build connections, think critically, and make decisions, because they now have a vested interest in the content. When students take on roles, whether as scientists, literary characters, historical figures, or famous artists, the content becomes richer because they apply their own emotions to making the characters come to life.

An equally important facet of our coaching philosophy is an emphasis on negotiating with students to determine reasonable expectations and criteria for assessment. It is important that students know exactly what is expected of them and how they need to perform. They should have a voice in their own learning, and a stake in their own assessment. As the assessment process becomes clearly defined and student goals are outlined and realized, cooperative groups will work more effectively with one another to solve problems.

Essential Questions and Guiding Questions and Statements

Each section of this book includes an essential question about the material covered and a list of guiding questions and statements related to the essential question. (In Section 1, you'll also find essential questions and guiding questions and statements at the beginning of each chapter.) Essential questions frame the material and promote higher-level thinking. They help link concepts and principles; because they relate to real problems in the classroom, they are anchored in the life of the reader. Essential questions promote deep and enduring understanding; they cannot be answered in one sentence. Though they are written simply, they are complex enough to be broken down into more specific guiding questions and statements. Heidi Hayes Jacobs refers to essential questions as "Mind Velcro": When you read each chapter, the information "sticks" to the essential question, which in turn helps the reader to synthesize the material into a deep, long-lasting understanding of the topic.

Overall Goal

Our overall goal is to ignite people's thinking and to be a catalyst for educational change. What would happen if superintendents coached principals, principals coached teachers, teachers coached students, and students coached their peers? A coaching environment would exist vertically as well as horizontally. Not only would skills resonate throughout the school, but they could also be extended to parent-teacher organizations, and from there to the students' homes.

With that being said, welcome to *Teachers as Classroom Coaches: How to Motivate Students Across the Content Areas*. We hope you enjoy testing and refining your own skills as much as we enjoyed testing and refining ours. After approximately 30 years of teaching, the techniques that we outline in this book have come to define us as educators as no other training has. Employing these techniques helped to improve our lives, our relationships, our teaching, and the way we view the world. We hope that you have the same experience.

Section 1

Creating the Coaching Environment

In this section, we define the art of coaching, describing in detail how teachers can empower and motivate students by giving them more responsibility, providing them with choices, enhancing their self-esteem, and relieving them of stress. We also discuss the conditions necessary for a productive atmosphere and explore how coaching helps teachers to determine the aptitude of students by recognizing their talents and grouping them accordingly. The teacher-coach becomes aware of the appropriateness of the content, matches it to an effective strategy, and uses that strategy to help students develop their skills.

Schools need not be institutions where learning stops at the classroom door; they can be vigorous centers bursting with creativity, intellectual engagement, and fun. Yes, fun! The goal of learning may be to expand the mind and better understand the world, but the road to getting there does not have to be straight and narrow—it can be an interconnected circle of lively and intelligent discussions, where knowledge bursts through the doors, the windows, the walls, and the floor, and every day there is something new to be discovered.

On the following page, you'll find an essential question and some guiding questions and statements to consider when reading chapters 1–7.

Essential Question: In what ways would the field of education benefit from coaching?

Guiding Questions and Statements:
- How can coaching lessen conflicts in the school?
- In what ways can coaching develop better listening skills?
- For what reasons do students perform better when coached?
- Describe in detail how coaching increases the ability to resolve conflicts.
- Explain specifically how coaching can encourage better organization and note-taking skills.
- How can coaching promote innovation and creativity?
- Describe in detail how coaching helps to overcome emotional and environmental roadblocks.
- How does allowing students ownership of their work empower them?
- Describe in detail how coaching improves cooperative group performance.
- How does a coaching environment decrease student, staff, and administrator absenteeism?
- In what ways does a coaching environment increase motivation and the passion to learn or perform one's duties?

Teacher-Coaches

Essential Question: What is coaching?

Guiding Questions and Statements:
- In what ways are coaching techniques motivational?
- Describe in detail how the environment changes due to a coaching environment.
- Why is student behavior modified in a coaching environment?
- For what reasons should students be trained to use coaching with each other in a coaching school?

* * *

There is nothing wrong with setting the stage for an activity or lesson with a 5- to 7-minute lecture. In fact, the shorter the better: Research has shown that students lose interest and focusing ability after the first 7 to 15 minutes of listening to a lecture (Bonwell & Eison, 1991). At the outset of a lesson, the main objective for any teacher is to set the stage by motivating students to engage enthusiastically in the day s activity.

Teachers who work as coaches have the same responsibilities as always, they just take a more interactive approach toward them. Like sports coaches, these teachers mix with everyone and are involved in everything. They motivate students to achieve results by instructing, guiding, and listening to them; when the going gets tough and enthusiasm wanes, they are there to show students the way. The classroom is the playing field, the students are the team, and the teacher, as the coach, holds everything together.

What Is Coaching?

More than 2,400 years ago, at the height of the Athenian enlightenment, Socrates asserted that teachers should help students to uncover information for themselves. This was a radical departure from the traditional approach of the time, which thought of students as empty vessels and of teachers as dispensers of information. Socrates' philosophy of teaching set the stage for coaching, which aims to unlock student potential.

Coaching is concerned with long-term skill development rather than with quick fixes or temporary understanding. We define coaches as those who offer inspiration, guidance, training, and modeling, and who enhance others' abilities through motivation and support (Longenecker & Pinkel, 1997). The goal of teachers who coach is to help students

- Find their inner strengths and passions in order to nurture self-worth and identity,
- Have a voice in their own learning and negotiate collectively with the teacher to create the goals and objectives,
- Passionately engage in talking content to increase memory retention and fuel motivation to learn, and
- Use their inner talents to bring their work to the highest level of scholarship attainable.

To better understand coaching, we can compare it to other professions. According to CoachPeople Training (2003), coaching is multidisciplinary and helps individuals move toward effective action by focusing on the present. A coach asks questions that provoke awareness, creating an environment for self-discovery. By contrast, therapists often look at the past to help patients understand the present; guidance counselors address personal problems and may recommend academic or career placement; consultants, who are usually experts in a given field, provide techniques and answers to questions; and mentors help individuals replace or take on specific new positions.

Coaches as Motivators

How do we motivate students? First, we need to develop a relationship of trust, based on a sense of security in a risk-free environment. Students need to feel that they can make new leaps in their endeavors within the security of this relationship. Second, teachers need to offer assignments that are intellectually challenging, but not overly difficult. The coach's ultimate goal is first to motivate students through guidance and activity, and then to tap the motivation inherent in students' natural curiosity.

Time and time again, research has shown that if students are truly engaged in learning, their recall increases (Conway, Cohen, & Stanhope, 1991; MacKenzie & White, 1982; Semb & Ellis, 1994; Surges, Ellis, & Wulfeck, 1981). For example, in a study of an accounting course, Specht and Sandlin (1991) found that role playing enhanced students' conceptual understanding more than did traditional lecturing. It is crucial, therefore, for teacher-coaches to motivate their students into activities that are as realistic as possible. Whether the forum is a debate, discussion, or simulation, students must feel that they are writing and researching for practical use.

To move into effective action, teacher-coaches must help students develop responsibility and choice, relieve stress, increase self-esteem and identity, and make real contributions to the classroom.

Developing Responsibility and Choice

It is a challenge to move towards a classroom environment where students have more responsibility and choice in their learning. Such a change might make students feel uncomfortable at first, as they are accustomed to the teacher telling them what to do. Because students who take more responsibility for their actions engage more proactively with classroom activities, teachers should coach students to determine their own goals. With responsibility comes accountability: Individuals are answerable for their choices and are evaluated accordingly. Therefore, the first step in helping students move into effective action is for the teacher to coach the students to take ownership of what needs to be accomplished.

Relieving Stress

With responsibility comes a certain degree of stress. Students have to uncover information themselves instead of letting the teacher dish it out. Teacher-coaches need to work with student groups to help ensure that their approach to the task at hand is manageable. We must help students to discover what is unknown for themselves (Dutton, 1997).

A changed environment can lead to a fear of the unknown, which in turn can lead to stress. Developing student responsibility gradually and having a plan of action in place can alleviate students' uncertainties.

Increasing Self-Esteem and Identity

As student responsibility and choice increase and stress levels decrease, students should have the opportunity to build self-esteem and identity. It is easy to imagine how empowered students might feel when using a new strategy in their own learning, especially when it is effective. The sense of accomplishment and independence that students feel after completing a job without being told what to do every step of the way is a reward in itself. Before the teacher knows it, students begin to mature emotionally as they realize that they have the power to make choices in their own learning. Teacher-coaches help their students become confident and competent in the learning environment (Hudson, 1999).

Making a Real Contribution

When teachers function as coaches, students move from writing reports for the teacher's eyes only to preparing projects, position papers, or perspectives for use in real-life simulations, discussions, or debates. Regardless of the forum, students feel they are making a real contribution for all to witness. When students engage in simulations, the teacher's job is to help them examine the ethics and values in the content. As in everyday life, our contributions are never purely academic.

● ● ●

When students reflect on the coaching model being used in the classroom, they feel more comfortable with the teacher's role as someone who is invested in their learning. Teachers help students to individually apply the content to their personal experiences; to quote O'Neil and Hopkins (2002), coaching "allow[s] the student-teacher relationship to develop on a deeper level . . . and provide[s] an opportunity for the teacher to step out of the expert mode and engage with the students in a process of co-inquiry" (p. 407).

Teacher-coaches model coaching techniques for students and discuss their meaning at every stage of development. The goal of school-based coaching is for the students to take on the roles of peer coaches with one another. We recommend hanging posters of coaching strategies in the classrooms to help students incorporate the language of coaching as they acquire essential skills. When students circulate from one classroom to another, they become aware that coaching is the culture of the school. Similar experiences in different classes reinforce and deepen individual understanding of coaching techniques.

2 Personality Types and Teaming

Essential Question: What does it mean to be part of a team?

Guiding Questions and Statements:
- Describe in detail the components of a well-functioning team.
- In what ways do personality types affect teaming?
- Explain specifically how talent can be fostered by teaming students more effectively.
- In what ways can team members assess themselves?

• • •

Much as sports coaches need to know what talents and attributes each player brings to a team, teachers need to know what aptitudes students bring with them to cooperative groups. Obviously, groups will need to be refined throughout the school year as the teacher gets to know the students well. Over time, the teacher will switch the students around to make the groups more effective.

Personality Types

When we refer to student talents and abilities, we mean the types of thinking aptitudes that students bring to the table—we are not discussing levels of achievement, though grouping by those criteria has merit at times. The teacher should get to know how the students operate: What are their strengths and weaknesses when working together? Let's examine some common student personality types and their respective aptitudes.

Managers

Students who fit this type are extremely focused, highly organized, and able to plan actions day by day. They may come to class with an organizer or daily planner, as they need a structured environment at all times. Managers have a natural ability to take charge; they like to move others into action. Sometimes Managers have unusually high expectations of others that may prove unrealistic.

Conductors

These students like to dole out responsibility. They enjoy networking and fostering alliances; like orchestra conductors, who are happiest when the musicians meld as one to play a piece perfectly, these students like to see the various members of their groups gel to complete their assigned goals. When all members of a group know exactly what they need to do, it is the Conductor who coordinates them into effective action.

Strategists

These students do not concern themselves with the organizational aspects of the work at hand, but rather with the strategies needed to get the work done. Strategists are motivated by thinking up alternative ways of accomplishing goals. They are able to differentiate tasks efficiently, which in turn helps them create work strategies.

Problem Solvers

These students avoid tension at all costs. They like to think things through by identifying problems and considering possible solutions. Problem Solvers keep their focus on the goal of the work, preventing it from being sidelined by distractions.

Creative Thinkers

These students have a different slant on the material at hand than do their peers; they are usually talented and can be counted on to be offbeat and original. Creative Thinkers may demonstrate their originality through wordplay, jokes, or even cynicism, but beneath the humor they will not hesitate to think outside the box. Often disorganized and prone to losing their way, Creative Thinkers look to others to bring their creative slants to productive ends.

Motivators

These students provide the group with incentive. They are persuasive and can get others to focus on taking action. Motivators are like cheerleaders: effervescent and outgoing, they help make group work more enjoyable.

Team Players

Though these students do not want the responsibility of organizing, problem solving, or motivating, they are eager to accept assigned chores and ready to complete their share of the workload. Team Players enjoy being a part of the group, receiving direction, and being told what is expected. They like the fact that their classmates consider them to be trustworthy and dependable.

Therapists

These students have a unique understanding of how to communicate information to others in a manner that is respectful and understanding of others' capabilities. Therapists can give direction to students who stumble or lose their way and can analyze where fellow group members are going wrong. You can depend on Therapists to check material and improve it; they are good at sharpening others' skills and constructively pointing out areas for improvement. They have a perceptive awareness of individual differences and can capitalize on strengths to help nurture areas of weakness. Most importantly, these students have the interpersonal skills to make others feel good about themselves.

● ● ●

We would never suggest that the above list is definitive, but we do hope that it provides a hint of what to expect from students. Principal Genevieve Stanislaus of New York City's Life Sciences Secondary School found the categorizations helpful. "Everybody has different strengths and weaknesses, and all the categories carry positive tones," she said. "I like how [the categorization] empowers students to be the most effective with the gifts they have."

Some students may fit perfectly into the confines of one specific category, while others may fit into two (or even three), and still others won't fit into any category at all. Still, the more teachers work at grouping students, the like-lier they'll be to say, at the conclusion of a unit, "That was a job well done."

Teacher-coaches shouldn't be surprised to find that some students need to be shuffled from one group to another for better balance. Creating effec-tive groups takes time and fine-tuning; good teachers will make changes throughout the year. As students grow and mature in the group environ-ment, their needs change accordingly. A good student-centered instruc-tor will be constantly aware of classroom dynamics. Teachers may be astounded at how quickly students develop in secondary schools, where the rate of emotional and cognitive growth is thrown into high gear.

If you wish to investigate personality types in greater depth, consider one of the many formal assessment tools on the market, such as Meyers-Briggs, MAPP, Platinum Rule, or Emotional Intelligence.

Teaming

When teachers find that students work well together, the classroom takes on a magical aura. As professionals, we instantly sense the difference between a high-functioning cooperative group and a low-functioning one. Quality of work is one indicator of how well the groups are working: Why does one group perform exceptionally while another simply struggles? Is it sheer luck and chemistry, or a determined effort and willingness on the part of certain students? What exactly defines a group that functions at a high level of efficiency?

Group success is certainly defined by individuals who, working together, establish clear priorities and understand their roles and respon-sibilities. These students foster an aura of inclusion, where each and every group member is welcomed and made to feel needed by the group. Members of high-functioning teams support one another emotionally through thick and thin, never dumping too much work on other members. If a particular group member's workload becomes unexpectedly burdensome, the group members all pull up their sleeves to help that student achieve her respon-sibility. Students are willing to take all the steps (and risks) necessary to attain their goals.

Successful cooperative groups also have excellent communication skills. Members offer constant feedback and suggestions to one another, and channels for dialogue are always open. Most importantly, they celebrate each other's achievements; after all, nothing is more inspiring than authentic praise.

Three Basic Goals of Teaming

As teacher-coaches, how do we guide our students so that they work in harmony as a single, dynamic unit, without neglecting their individual strengths? Let's examine three basic goals of teaming: inclusion, assertion, and cooperation.

Inclusion. It is extremely important for teacher-coaches to make sure that all group members feel a sense of inclusion, as though they each have something to give to the team. If a handful of students dominate the group and ignore the other members, then a low-functioning group will develop. Although different students have different strengths, teachers should take care not to always assign students the same roles, as this can prevent the students from developing other skills. When teachers rotate student roles and ask members to help each other, they equalize the students' expectations of what is required of them over the long haul. At this stage, the energy is directed towards one another as they all find a sense of belonging.

Assertion. Some teachers may not realize that some roles may be more or less burdensome than others. When students see themselves as task managers, they are free to assert themselves by asking other students to chip in when necessary. For example, if the teacher has assigned one student to be the group "paper cutter" during a map-making exercise, the student could enlist fellow group members to help with the task rather than cut all the paper himself.

Cooperation. The goals of inclusion and assertion cannot be accomplished unless group members understand that they must support and cooperate with one another. At the same time, teachers should help students understand that cooperation does not mean losing a sense of self or of one's role in the group. Although the most productive teams are highly cooperative, a little tension can be positive in that it gives students a competitive edge and sparks them into action. In truly cooperative groups, the interests of individual group members are all pulled toward a common goal, which becomes the focus of their energy.

Team Assessment

Team assessment allows students to identify their strengths and weaknesses so that they can focus on completing their tasks. Teacher-coaches can set the stage by explaining that the way we see ourselves is not neces-

Figure 2.1

Individual Team Assessment Chart

Scoring Guide 1 = not at all 2 = somewhat 3 = usually 4 = all the time	Environment	enthusiastic	friendly	unselfish	Communication	sharing	speaks his/her mind appropriately	honest	good listener	tolerant of other people's weaknesses	problem solver
Lashawn											
Pablo											
Tina											
Timmy											

Scoring Guide 1 = not at all 2 = somewhat 3 = usually 4 = all the time	Productivity	organized	cooperative	supportive	committed to the task	works well with others	reliable	patient	adaptable	creative	trustworthy
Lashawn											
Pablo											
Tina											
Timmy											

sarily the way others do, and then having students rate both themselves and their fellow group members on a chart according to a scale of 1 to 4 (see Figure 2.1). Criteria for assessment may include (but are not limited to) the following areas: cooperation, support, trustworthiness, reliability, patience, friendliness, commitment to the task, enthusiasm, working well with others, tolerance of other people's weaknesses, sharing, selflessness, and adaptability.

Students should begin by rating themselves on the chart, then setting it aside. Next, the teacher should distribute another copy of the same chart and have every student rate her fellow group members. (The teacher can also use the same chart to rate the students.) Once all students have privately rated both themselves and each other, the students hand the second chart over to the teacher, keeping the first one to themselves. The teacher then tallies the results and gives the students the group averages for each criterion. Now the students can compare their self-assessments on the first chart to the group averages. The averages make it difficult for the students to blame any particular person for a weak rating in any of the areas. Students can be encouraged to write an evaluation of how their peers see them as opposed to how they see themselves. (See Figure 5.1 in Chapter 5 for an additional form that teachers can use to assess group progress.)

Listening and Questioning Skills 3

Essential Questions:
- What does it mean to be an effective listener?
- What is guided listening?

Guiding Questions and Statements:
- In what ways do we listen at different levels?
- Compare and contrast the differences between good listening and guided listening.
- Explain in detail how teachers can assess how a team is functioning.
- Describe specifically how teachers can approach teams for coaching purposes.
- Compare and contrast the differences between negative questioning and supportive questioning.
- In what ways can we guide students through supportive questioning?
- Describe in detail the difference between simple questioning and exploratory questioning.
- In what ways do we gain information by implementing contextual listening?
- Explain in detail the role of the teacher during contextual listening.

• • •

Once a spirit of teamwork has been established in the classroom, the teacher's next objective is to build awareness of students' potential for productivity and cooperation. When teachers make careful listening and critical analysis priorities, they are able to ensure greater clarity of perception among students. This clarity can be achieved by focusing on pertinent information that students express while disregarding the superfluous. Student awareness of group dynamics, relationships between themselves and the content, and their emotional and psychological states can help students to coach one another in groups.

Supportive Questions and Comments

The power of words goes a long way. The way in which we speak or write can either open or close doors when communicating with students. Every question or statement can be phrased in a positive way. In Figure 3.1, compare the negative question starters on the left to the positive ones on the right. Notice which ones allow for student ownership of the decision-making process.

Figure 3.1
Negative vs. Positive Questions and Comments

Negative	Positive
You are required to . . .	Consider . . .
You need to consider . . .	May I suggest that you consider . . .
	How might you look at this differently?
Why didn't you . . .	Explain in detail what happened so that we can better understand your idea . . .
I noticed that you failed . . .	Now that you know that doesn't work, what other options . . .
You should think about . . .	You may want to think about . . .
You could . . .	In what ways could you . . .
What were you thinking when . . .	Describe in detail what specifically happened when . . .
You're not doing it right.	May I offer a suggestion that might make your task easier?

Simple vs. Exploratory Questions

Just as we can change negative questions to positive ones, we can also change simple questions to exploratory ones (see Figure 3.2). Although simple questions can be appropriate for use with individual students, exploratory questions (also known as probing questions) are more appropriate for use with the entire class, as they invariably generate clearer and deeper responses. As ESL teacher Richard Ciriello of New York City's Lower East Side Preparatory School pointed out, exploratory questions are "very effective for getting the students to think more about the topic."

The COACH Model

We have created the COACH Model to help teachers use exploratory questions. As a coach, the teacher's objective is to elicit responses that reflect how well the group or student is progressing. The questions should be open-ended, probing for as much detail and description as possible.

Figure 3.2
Simple vs. Exploratory Questions and Comments

Simple	Exploratory
You are required to . . .	Consider ...
What will you do?	*Describe in detail* what you will do.
Why did you do that?	*For what reasons* did you do that?
How can you accomplish this task?	*Generate a list* of what you can do to accomplish this task.
When did this happen?	*Explain when specifically* this happened.
What did other people think?	*In what ways* can you describe what happened from the different perspectives of those who were there?
Are these items different?	*Compare and contrast* what makes these items similar and what makes them different.

"Using COACH questions is a good way to determine that students understand tasks and work completely and thoroughly," said Kim Tretter, who teaches 10th and 11th grades at Life Sciences Secondary School. "It also helps the teacher to see where students need work and which students need extra clarification or attention."

The COACH acronym stands for the following:

C = Clarity of the task. Is the task at hand clear to students? (Example: "Please explain to me in your own words what you need to accomplish. Explain specifically what you have decided to do.")

O = Ownership of the task. Do the students feel a sense of ownership and responsibility for the task, or are they just trying to secure a passing grade? (Example: "How have you decided to divide the responsibility? For what reasons do you feel that this is fair, in terms of workload?")

A = Attention to others. Are the students attentive to one another and aware of how their group is functioning? (Example: "Please share with me what you have been able to accomplish thus far today. Describe in detail how well you think you are working as a group. In what ways is this relevant to what you are trying to achieve together?")

C = Comprehension of the content. Do the students understand the content? Are they comfortably engaged, or is the content either too easy or too difficult? (Example: "Please show me where you found this information, because I find it fascinating. Please also explain the most important points that you found in your research. For what reasons does this information make sense to you? For what reasons do you think you can make the connection between the research and the lesson?")

H = Heightened or hidden emotions. Are student emotions set at a comfortable level? (Example: "I noticed that there is very little discussion at this table. Please share with me how you feel your group is functioning right now. It appears that this group has divided itself into pairs. Please describe what has taken place.")

Exploratory questions can inspire students to probe deeper rather than becoming defensive when they feel inadequate. By engaging teacher-coaches in the inquiry process, exploratory questions convey the fact that teachers are not the sole repositories of all knowledge, and that they are interested primarily in their students' projects.

Teachers can assess how well they ask questions by evaluating themselves on a continuous basis. We have modified the guidelines provided by Elder and Paul (2002) to evaluate teacher questions for clarity, precision, logic, relevance, accuracy, significance, depth, and fairness. Teacher-coaches may ask themselves the questions in Figure 3.3 to guide and reflect upon their ability to ask students meaningful questions. Figure 3.4 presents a list of sample questions and statements for each of the factors being assessed.

Figure 3.3

Teacher Self-Assessment for Asking Students Questions

Did my questions . . .

- Appear clear and to the point, empowering the students to think of possibilities? (Clarity)
- Provide enough detail, so that everyone understood what I was asking? (Precision)
- Flow in an orderly fashion? Did I make the right connections from one point to the next? (Logic)
- Stay focused and consistent with the main objective? (Relevance)
- Encourage students to check for validity and correctness? (Accuracy)
- Bring out the most significant points or concepts? (Significance)
- Allow students to probe their thinking, encouraging deeper thought of complex issues? (Depth)
- Appear open enough, not showing bias towards one viewpoint or another? (Fairness)

Taking the time to pose appropriate questions or statements allows teacher-coaches to put themselves in the students' place during lessons. As students take risks and attempt new endeavors, teachers should guide them and facilitate their learning in a positive fashion. By prompting students with questions that initiate scholarship, teachers allow students to think critically and apply multiple perspectives to their research. When teachers abandon such formulations as "could have" or "should have" and replace them with "May I suggest . . . ," "You may want to consider . . . ," or "In what ways can you . . ." ownership and responsibility of the material shift from the teacher to the students.

Figure 3.4

Sample Questions and Comments for Assessing Essential Factors

The following questions and comments can help teacher-coaches check for clarity, precision, logic, relevance, accuracy, significance, depth, and fairness:

- I heard you say . . . ; did I understand you correctly? (Clarity)
- Please be more specific or give an example so I can understand you precisely. (Precision)
- For what reasons does this information make sense to you? (Logic)
- In what ways is this relevant to what you are trying to achieve? (Relevance)
- Please show me where you found this information, because it is fascinating. (Accuracy)
- Please explain the most important points that you found in your research. (Significance)
- For what reasons do you think you can make the connection? (Depth)
- Describe in detail how you were able to put your own bias on hold while taking this oppositional viewpoint. (Fairness)

Contextual Listening Skills

Good teacher-coaches are always patient, supportive, attentive, genuinely interested, and aware of what is important in a lesson. For this to be the case, coaches must remain somewhat detached from the activities at hand; rather than take ownership of the process, they should allow students to make their way on their own. When moving from group to group, teacher-coaches should take careful notes, both to help the groups on a continual basis and to keep track of which groups they've visited. Of course, coaches should be seen as teachers as well—in command of the classroom and possessed of knowledge and expertise. They need to know when to share knowledge and when to withhold it. Coaches must also possess an unflinching belief in their students' ability to uncover content and complete their work with relative ease.

When assessing how students talk and act in groups, we might examine such criteria as eye contact, respectfulness, and effective use of content. Contextual listening helps teachers *and* students read between the lines to assess these factors.

The 3 Ps + C Model

The 3 Ps + C Model can help teachers "gain entry" to student work during lessons.

P = Permission. Coaches should ask for students' permission to offer help (e.g., "May I join you for a few minutes?" "May I offer a suggestion?"). In this way, the teacher-coach adroitly avoids angering the student. When asking for permission, teacher-coaches should use polite, unobtrusive language.

P = Purpose. Once the task is introduced, teacher-coaches should convey its purpose (e.g., "I would like to discuss your project with all of you." "Tell me a bit more as to why you would like to do . . ."). Again, questions should be polite and unobtrusive. In conveying the task's purpose, coaches also describe the steps that the task will require.

P = Positive. Offering students suggestions and support, the teacher-coach phrases as politely as possible (e.g., "How can I can help you with what you're doing?" "May I offer a short reading in this book that might help you with the problem?"). The students can then decide whether or not to accept the suggestions and take ownership of the work.

C = Compliment. Teacher-coaches should compliment students on the progress they've made and the work they're doing (e.g., "You all have the necessary abilities and you can be creative." "It's great to see you cooperating, and the continuing dialogue is wonderful.").

The GELVE Model of Contextual Listening

We've designed the GELVE Model to help teachers remember what to look for during contextual listening: gremlins, eye contact, body language, voice inflection, and emotions. "One thing I love about this approach is that you begin to listen with your eyes," said Life Sciences Secondary School teacher Libby Wickes. "It allows you to extend the dialogue while the focus remains on the student."

G = Gremlins. Teacher-coaches need to listen for the little fears that haunt the recesses of our minds. These inner voices, which Carlson (2003) calls "gremlins," make us nervous, hesitant, opposed to change, and wary of the unknown—characteristics that can make it difficult for students to move forward. Students at various stages of development struggle to overcome the voices that say, "You're not ready," "You can't do this," "It's too difficult," "You're not strong enough," and "You're not smart enough." During contextual listening, teacher-coaches should help students understand and face their gremlins.

E = Eye contact. When engaging with students, teacher-coaches need to be 100 percent tuned in. Eye contact should consist of meaningful connections, rather than a random gaze in the students' direction. When talking one-on-one with the teacher, do students make eye contact or avert their eyes? There may be a volume of unsaid emotions in the eyes turning away.

L = (Body) language. Teacher-coaches should hone in on body language as well as on words. For example, students who sit in a relaxed position with arms and legs uncrossed project a level of comfort with the activity at hand, whereas those whose legs are crossed and arms are folded might be uncomfortable and resistant to the work. Students who cover their mouths while speaking might feel anxiety and trepidation. When students are excited about their work, they might lean forward toward others in the group. When deciding which group to visit first, teacher-coaches might scan the room for body language cues. There are times when body language is much more reliable than the spoken word; when approaching each group or student, teachers should lend greater weight to body language than to verbal cues.

Teacher-coaches must pay attention to their own body language as well. When approaching a group, they should lean forward or even squat down to the students' level, melding into the activity. Being at the same eye level as students sends the message that all parties in the dialogue are equally important.

Coaches should teach students how to read body language in groups. This is important for effective cooperative group interactions.

V = Voice inflection. The inflection and tone of voice of teacher-coaches differ with every situation. Because their objectives are to motivate students and raise their awareness, coaches should use vigorous and spirited voices, as well as positive inflections that help boost student egos and increase self-esteem. Students' tones of voice can supply information that is not being communicated in the words that they use; by paying attention to students' modulation and pitch, coaches can get some idea of where the conversation is going. A student who has an unusual, rapid speech pattern coupled with a higher tone may communicate anxiety.

E = Emotions. When students work together, their interactions often tap their emotions. When emotions are positive, this works to the group's advantage; when they are negative, however, they can be a burden. Teacher-coaches should scan the room and hone in on students who appear to be upset or distancing themselves from the others. In these situations, coaches may inquire about the cause for anxiety or apprehension. Sometimes students become uncomfortable for reasons that have nothing to do with their scholastic aptitude.

In especially sensitive situations, coaches should remove upset students from their groups and speak to them one-on-one before addressing the group as a whole. Although students may claim that nothing is wrong in front of other group members, they will talk more openly in private (See Chapter 6 for more on one-on-one coaching.) When trying to read students' emotions, teachers should watch for body language cues.

Teacher-Coach Behaviors During Contextual Listening

Teacher-coaches should practice reflective response and self-assessment during contextual listening, and should always keep their focus on the students.

Reflective response. Students are always quick to pick up how engaged teachers really are in their learning. After students have discussed their group plans in detail, teacher-coaches should reflect upon and repeat what has been said. This technique is meaningful for two reasons: It communicates to students that the coach is really listening for content and that their endeavors are being seriously considered, and it clarifies the group's plans for both the students and the teacher. Reflective response allows students either to acknowledge that the teacher understands what they've said, or, if they have been misinterpreted, to clarify what they meant.

Once both parties acknowledge their mutual understanding, the teacher-coach should take notes on what was discussed. The interaction between teacher and students is thus chiseled in stone, allowing the teacher to reread it before returning to the group in the future.

Self-assessment. Teacher-coaches need to assess their own performance from time to time. At the secondary level, it is easy for teachers to be excited about the content because it was what they majored in at school, and certain sections of the curriculum will be more appealing than others. At the primary level, however, teachers teach all content areas, only a fraction of which will be personally exciting to them. Regardless, teacher-coaches should regularly assess their behavior to ensure that they are not transferring their own dislike of certain content areas to the students.

During their self-assessment, teacher-coaches should revisit how well the students learned the content of a given lesson, whether or not the strategies used allowed the students to go deeper and apply more meaning to the content, whether or not students had the skills to complete their assigned tasks, and how well all three areas were integrated into the lesson. Part of contextual listening is the teacher's ability, working as a coach, to assess what is happening while being engaged with students.

Keeping the focus on students. Teachers are often inclined to lead students down predetermined paths. A teacher-coach will stay attuned to the interests of the students, as long as they are progressing logically toward the intended goal. In such cases, after the students have reached their objectives, explored all their options, and compiled all their ideas and thoughts, the teacher might ask if students are open to hearing some of *his* thoughts. However, if the coach sees that students are wandering off track, he should immediately intercede and ask, "In what ways does this relate to what we were discussing?" The coach seizes that exact moment and steps in to guide the students before it's too late. To ensure that students are staying focused, the coach may have to rotate from group to group more often. (This is especially important with younger students, who tend to be more easily distracted.)

Case Study of Contextual Listening and the 3 Ps + C Model

The following case study provides an example of how to apply contextual listening strategies in class. Strategies and key behaviors are noted in brackets.

• • •

Colby Jackson was a good student, and his homework was always meticulous and on time. Colby's uncle was a cartoonist, so Mr. Augustino was not surprised that his assignments were often accompanied by well-drawn illustrations. While in his reading group, Colby always joined his peers in choral readings. He appeared well adjusted and would even come to school when sick because he did not like to feel as if he'd missed anything. Colby had two good friends in class, Marcus and Jesse, who sat next to him. The three of them were like peas in a pod, and the bond extended beyond school.

One day, when Mr. Augustino announced that everyone would be assigned new reading group seats, Colby began to act out and kick a chair [*body language*]. Both Marcus and Jesse tried to console him, but Colby just pushed his close buddies away. Mr. Augustino was perplexed; he expected aggressive behavior from other students in his class, but certainly not from Colby. He took Colby to the library corner with the big beanbags and asked him to sit there and collect himself. Colby held his head down with his hands [*body language*].

After assigning a task to the rest of the class, Mr. Augustino approached Colby privately, using a quiet voice. He told Colby that he appeared to be pretty upset about something [*reflective response*], and Colby replied that he didn't want to lose his two good friends. Looking down while punching the beanbag [*body language*], Colby explained tearfully [*voice inflection*] that he was upset with himself for losing control and kicking the chair. The more upset he became, the harder it was to hold back the tears of frustration [*emotions*]; he did not want the rest of the class to think he was a crybaby [*emotions*]. Mr. Augustino told Colby that it's okay to sometimes cry, and not to worry. He told Colby that while it was only natural to feel threatened in situations where his friends might question his behavior, true friends would soon forget about it. After all, everyone has their moments of weakness.

When Mr. Augustino questioned Colby about school, Colby answered that he loved his friends, liked his teacher a lot, and loved math. When Mr. Augustino asked about reading, he noticed that Colby crossed his arms and looked away [*body language*], murmuring that it was "just okay" [*voice inflection*].

Mr. Augustino told Colby that he wasn't going to change his seat today, but could Colby join him for lunch [*permission*]? Colby agreed. (This was not unusual, as Mr. Augustino had lunch with a different student each week.)

As the students worked on their assigned tasks, Mr. Augustino reflected on everything he could recall about Colby. Two out of the past five times that Colby was asked to go to the board, he asked to go to the bathroom instead. Mr. Augustino tried to remember what subject areas were being covered when Colby excused himself. When called upon during math time, Colby always had his hand up. The one time Mr. Augustino had asked Colby to read aloud in the library corner, Colby asked that Mr. Augustino read first because he liked the sound of his "radio voice." A fire drill interrupted the class, and Colby didn't have the opportunity to read. These incidents did not register with Mr. Augustino until today. Could Colby have been hiding a gremlin that hindered him? Was his gremlin a weakness in his ability to read?

Mr. Augustino's curiosity was aroused. He knew his theory was pure speculation, but decided to put it to the test by calling for reading circle time just before lunch. During the reading circle time, he made note of the fact that Colby would look down at his book when Mr. Augustino looked at him, or at a peer when Mr. Augustino asked a question [*body language*].

During lunch, Mr. Augustino told Colby that he really liked having him as a student and that he was a great kid [*compliment*]. Then he decided to go out on a limb and tell Colby that he knew he was hiding something about reading. Because it was just the two of them, it was okay to talk about things in the open [*purpose*]. Mr. Augustino began to ask probing questions that would lead Colby to disclose his fears. He told Colby that he had his best interests at heart, and that Colby could trust him to be a good listener.

"Your worksheets are always perfect," he said. "You always draw nice pictures, and you always participate in choral readings [*compliment*]. But when I single you out to read or to write something on the board, you shy away. It appears that you may have trouble with reading [*purpose*]. In what ways did you succeed in fooling me? I'm impressed with the strategies that you used to trick everyone. Only a very smart person could pull that off [*compliment*]."

Colby was stunned. The thing he was hiding for so long was just brought out in the open, and no one was angry with him. His peers weren't around, so he didn't feel embarrassed. Surprisingly enough, his teacher was complimenting him on what a good trickster he was.

Now a bit prouder, Colby told all. "Well, Mr. Augustino, it's easy to copy my work off of Jesse because his handwriting is neat and large."

Mr. Augustino responded, "You selected Jesse because you knew he was a fine student and that his homework would be good enough to copy. Your gut served you well in this case [*reflective response*]."

"Yeah," said Colby, "and I use the pictures in reading circles because any dummy can follow the story by finding the clues in the drawings."

"With your family's background, I bet you see a lot more details in drawings than most kids [*reflective response*]," said Mr. Augustino. "But tell me, what about choral reading?"

"Well, Mr. Augustino, I sit next to Marcus, not only because we've known each other since we were born, but because he has such a great loud voice during choral reading. I just move my lips a little slower to what I hear him saying. It's easy, really."

At this point, Mr. Augustino said that he wanted to start meeting with Colby so that he could privately give him some tips on becoming a better reader [*purpose*]. He empathized with Colby, knowing how difficult it must be to cover up his gremlin.

"Describe what it was like to cover up this secret [*reflective response*]," he said. "In what ways was it hard on you? Or was it fairly easy?"

"I didn't like it much," replied Colby. "I was always nervous [*emotions*]. I think I was more nervous about the secret than worried about what I was supposed to read." Colby spoke in a low voice [*voice inflection*], and his shoulders were hunched [*body language*].

"This must be a very big weight that you've just lifted off your shoulders," said Mr. Augustino. "After learning some reading strategies, you will soon be able to relax and not have to worry about having this secret [*purpose*]. If you could either keep your secret or work to eliminate it, which would you choose?"

Colby's limbs were as limp as a rag doll's. He was exhausted. "I'd love to stamp it out forever," he said.

"Okay," said Mr. Augustino. "In order to spare you further embarrassment, would you like to meet with me so we can create a plan to help you with your reading [*permission*]?"

Colby agreed to meet with Mr. Augustino again to work out a plan of action. At the next meeting, Mr. Augustino said, "Colby, if you were in my place, what would you do to help determine where a student needs help with reading?"

"Like . . . make a list or something?" answered Colby.

"That's a great idea [*compliment*]," said Mr. Augustino. "I'll give you an example and then you can add to the list. How about I ask you to read something out loud to give me some clues as to where things might be difficult? How comfortable are you with this idea [*positive suggestion/support*]?"

"We're alone, so that's fine," Colby replied.

"Can we write it down?" asked Mr. Augustino [*permission*].

Colby nodded.

"Now, once again, if you were the teacher what else could be done?"

"I guess you could have me write something or test me on something."

"Those are two excellent ideas [*compliment*]. Let's add them to the list [*reflective response*]."

"But I don't want to be embarrassed by my friends. Please promise me that you won't do these things in front of them in class," Colby said, looking down anxiously [*eye contact*].

Mr. Augustino comforted Colby. "I can do even better than that," he said. "I can arrange a time for Ms. Wong, the reading specialist, to give you some tests in private, away from the classroom [*positive suggestion/support*]. We can all work together, if that's okay with you [*permission*].

"Our 10 minutes are up right now. So, how about I arrange with Ms. Wong to meet us here tomorrow so that I can introduce you to her [*permission*]?"

"Is she nice?" asked Colby. "Will she be upset that it's her lunch period?"

"All I can do is ask her permission to introduce you for a minute or two. I won't leave, I'll be here the whole time. It's really up to her. And yes, she's a really nice lady." Mr. Augustino smiled.

"Okay, but only for a couple of minutes."

At this point, Mr. Augustino notified his principal of the situation, and determined to meet with Colby's parents at the earliest opportunity to ask their permission to test Colby on his reading.

• • •

Mastering the concept of contextual listening brings teacher-coaches to a higher plane, for it enables them to engage in true dialogue with students. Dialogue signals a mutual respect—it creates an atmosphere where students feel that their words are relevant and actually being heard. Dialogue is not argumentative, but egalitarian; the coach and students meet on common ground and engage in an intellectual discourse that enhances the work in progress, further compounding the trust so essential to the coach-student relationship. Dialogue allows freedom of expression and engenders understanding and clarity, especially when questions probe the validity of what is being said. Here in its simplest format is the search for truth, where individuals share their points of view and display a willingness to be swayed. The teacher-coach who engages in contextual listening and actively embraces dialogue shows a commitment to learning at the highest level.

Levels of Listening

Mr. Augustino was an excellent listener: He was able to read all of Colby's signals and help him with his reading. What makes a teacher-coach a good listener? Figure 3.5 shows the four levels of listening.

Guided Listening

Teacher-coaches use guided listening when responding to students. Sometimes, students are stuck and need help moving forward to complete the task at hand; other times, they just need to be acknowledged. Let's examine some of the guided listening skills that the Institute for Professional Empowerment Coaching (2005) recommends.

Acknowledging. Letting students know that they've been heard is a powerful tool. Teacher-coaches should reflect what students say by paraphrasing their words. The dialogue lets coaches show that they have listened to and understood the students.

Figure 3.5

The Four Levels of Listening

Level 1: The teacher is not really listening or engaged.

Student: May I change my seat?

Teacher: Don't bother me with petty details.

Level 2: The teacher is listening, but doing so subjectively (i.e., from her point of view).

Student: May I change my seat?

Teacher: I once asked my teacher to switch my seat, but I learned that you can't always get what you want.

Level 3: The teacher is listening from the student's point of view.

Student: May I change my seat?

Teacher-Coach: You feel that you need your seat changed. Tell me what is bothering you.

Level 4: The teacher is listening from the student's point of view and picking up on intuitive cues.

Student: May I change my seat?

Teacher-Coach: Something is upsetting you so much that you want your seat changed. You appear anxious as you keep looking over your shoulders.

Student: I keep looking for books that would help me prepare, but they seem too difficult.

Teacher-Coach: You can't seem to find anything at the workstation that is at a comfortable reading level.

Student: To set up this experiment, I need a midsized beaker.

Teacher-Coach: In other words, the beakers that are available are not the correct size.

Clarifying. When a student expresses a thought that appears vague or unclear, the teacher-coach should ask the student to provide more detailed

information. Questioning for clarification also prods students to think independently.

Student: The serf needs to grow crops and give one-fifth to the king.
Teacher-Coach: What do you mean by "give one-fifth"?
Student: He has to figure out how much one-fifth of his crops is.
Teacher-Coach: Please explain why he needs to do that.
Student: It was his way of paying taxes.

Validating. When emotions affect the learning environment, it is important
for a teacher-coach to recognize students' feelings in a nonjudgmental
way. This allows students to know that the coach sees the world from their
perspective.

Student: I'm really upset that I wasn't chosen for the solo part in the county
chorus.
Teacher-Coach: It is very normal to have those feelings. You practiced hard
and you put all your efforts into trying out.

Reframing. Students can often understand a situation better when the
teacher-coach reframes it. Let's step out of the content area and use an
example of an older brother talking to his sister's teacher.

Brother: We are having trouble with Marcia at home. She is wearing heavy
make-up and tearing her jeans. I hope she is not a distraction in class.
Teacher-Coach: Many adolescent girls go through this stage. So much so,
that there are tons of books on the market addressing the fact. Marcia is
not the only one—as a matter of fact, she's in the mainstream.
Brother: Really? She's not the only one?
Teacher-Coach: Not by any stretch of the imagination. Think of it as a good
sign: If Marcia weren't testing the waters and breaking away from you and
your parents at this stage, she might do it at a later time, when it wouldn't be
so common. The fact that she's separating from all of you means that you've
given her all the basics that she needs. You've been a good brother and I'm
sure your parents are fine people.

Brother: But it's so difficult . . .

Teacher-Coach: No one ever said that adolescence was easy—not for them, and certainly not for you. You and your parents may want to go to the bookstore and review the many available books on this subject. They will give you some guidance on how to better understand and deal with this stage of development.

Growing. The teacher-coach works with students to change negative experiences into positive ones. Those with a truly positive attitude toward learning believe that even failure can be rewarding, as lessons learned can lead to greater success.

Student: I'm frustrated! I tried to build a paper Roman archway, but it can't hold any solid weight.

Teacher-Coach: It can be upsetting to find that a design you hoped would work didn't pan out. However, turn this experience around—start fresh with a new or modified design. What powerful information have you gained that can help you design something more successful?

Bottom lining. Sometimes students ramble, telling every unnecessary detail of a story. Teacher-coaches should interrupt rambling students to ask questions that help them focus on the matter at hand.

Student: I went to Molly's group but they are using the thermometer. I went to Hector's group and they won't let me borrow theirs because they are just about to use it. I went to—

Teacher-Coach: Melinda, what are you trying to tell me about your group and your thermometer?

Student: We broke it by accident.

Breaking resistance. Sometimes, a task that seems easy to one student may be overwhelming for another. When appropriate, teacher-coaches should work with students to determine their fears and break down the task into manageable steps. This allows students to focus on the problem from a fresh perspective.

Teacher-Coach: You appear turned off from the group.

Student: Nothing I do can please them.

Teacher-Coach: It's hard when you don't feel heard or appreciated. For what reasons do you feel this way?

Student: Because they're constantly on my case. I don't feel good when I'm around them.

Teacher-Coach: Describe specifically what they are asking you to do.

Student: To write neater, but I can't.

Teacher-Coach: Okay, so your penmanship isn't the best for their display. What else could you do?

Student: I don't know.

Teacher-Coach: How have you overcome this in the past?

Student: I could rap.

Teacher-Coach: So, you're a singer. What do people like about your rapping?

Student: I'm good with telling a story.

Teacher-Coach: Well, that's one great option. What's another?

Student: I guess I could type it on the computer.

Teacher-Coach: Now you're giving yourself some choices.

Student: Maybe if I tell them I'll create the rap from scratch, I could have one of them write it up any way they want!

Teacher-Coach: It sounds like it's time for you to go back to the group and negotiate.

Students coaching each other can learn to listen with the same degree of concentration as teacher-coaches. Deyshawn Thomas, a 10th grader who participated in coach training at Life Science Secondary School, commented that "[coaching] helped me to fully comprehend what my peer was asking me."

4 Coached Assessment

Essential Question: How does negotiation play a role in the classroom?

Guiding Questions and Statements:
- For what reasons is a teacher a negotiator?
- Explain in detail how a teacher instills ownership in a lesson.
- In what ways can the criteria for assessments be negotiated?
- Describe in detail the different ways assessment can be used in the classroom.

• • •

Coached assessment is a new and unique approach to evaluating student achievement. It helps students to demonstrate their knowledge and skills and teacher-coaches to evaluate classroom practices and procedures. Commonly associated with project-based learning, coached assessment allows teachers to both coach and assess students. This process can take place before, during, and after their work on simulations; in discussion groups and debate teams; during science experiments; and while creating portfolios and other projects. When teachers and students outline the content and skills to be learned and the expectations for learning ahead of time, the stage is set for effective teacher-student communication. When students are fully engaged in helping the teacher determine the criteria of assessment, the quality of their work is bound to soar.

Teacher-coaches should modify the criteria for assessment on an ongoing basis to reflect their coaching methods and better meet the needs of the students. In doing so, they should ask themselves the following questions:

- Do the strategies and the materials meet expectations?
- Are the students progressing at the expected pace?
- Are the students using the content effectively and taking ownership of it for personal use?

Types of coached assessment may vary from class to class and day to day, depending on the students' needs. Teacher-coaches need to adequately pinpoint the necessary skills to be learned without ever losing sight of the students' levels of emotional or social development. To ascertain whether or not an instructional strategy is working, the teacher-coach should examine the following four areas:

1. Content. How well do the students understand the material within the context of the strategy or forum used? Are students so thoroughly engrossed in the unit that the strategy or forum makes sense? Do students have the necessary background for more in-depth work?

2. Strategy. How well does the strategy or forum bring the content to life? Do students understand what is expected of them? Are they able to prepare properly for the work ahead?

3. Skills. Does the strategy or forum strengthen students' skills? Is it too easy or too hard for them? In what ways does the teacher need to modify practices to best meet the needs of the students?

4. Combination. Do the content, strategy, and skills intertwine in a way that helps students to succeed?

Negotiable Contracting of Assessment Criteria

Though negotiable contracting may sound better suited to labor disputes than to the classroom, it's actually a terrific way to get students involved in setting the criteria on which their grades will be determined. Adaptable to all content areas and flexible enough to accommodate most types of learning, negotiable contracting is currently being implemented in many classrooms.

Teachers may at first be wary of asking students for input into their assessment, fearing that they may take advantage and set very low standards. This seldom occurs, however; when asked to suggest assessment criteria, students are surprisingly responsible and thoughtful (Stix, 2002). Students who are appropriately coached can often pinpoint just what they think is important to learn in a given unit.

Allowing students to help set assessment criteria makes them more willing to accept responsibility for the grades they receive, and motivates them to do the best they can to meet their own goals. Students thus do not view grades as arbitrarily bestowed gifts or punishments: If a student gets a grade of 86 out of 100 on a project, she can refer to the list of criteria and their respective values to see exactly why 14 points were deducted. With this understanding, students are better able to critique both themselves and each other.

Once an assignment has been clearly explained, the teacher-coach should ask students to put themselves in the teacher's place. What criteria do they think should be used for grading their work? The teacher and students should negotiate the goals until a final agreement is reached that is acceptable to all parties (Stix, 2000). During the negotiation, the teacher should explain what she thinks should be included in the assessment, to ensure that no important area is overlooked. It is essential that the guidelines be made available to everyone, whether on a handout or in some conspicuous and accessible place in the classroom, so that students can refer to them as they proceed through the unit of study.

Determining Assessment Criteria During Negotiable Contracting

To determine the criteria for assessment during negotiable contracting, the teacher-coach needs to ask students to

- Identify the assignment.
- List the most salient points of the assignment.
- Discuss how they will know that the content has been "uncovered" or properly researched.
- Explain what it means to work with one another productively.
- Consider how their behavior while undertaking the assignment will affect the results.

When determining assessment criteria for group work, the following steps should be followed:

1. Each student brainstorms a list of criteria privately.

2. After a specified amount of time, the students in each group pool their lists into a single master list.

3. Each group narrows its master list down to five criteria.

4. Group members arrange the five chosen criteria in order of importance, hoping that they will be the first to share an essential idea.

5. Addressing the whole class, the teacher asks that each group offer one assessment criterion. As each group does so, the teacher writes the criterion on the board. When every group has spoken, the process is repeated, until all the criteria are listed.

6. The teacher works with the class to prioritize the list of criteria on the board.

7. The teacher reviews the list. If there are important criteria that no group has mentioned, the teacher can add them to the list as nonnegotiable items.

8. The teacher and students discuss which of the criteria are most salient, and how many should be selected. (We recommend four to six criteria for most assignments.)

9. The final list is arranged in order of importance.

10. The teacher and students discuss how much each criterion is worth. (For example, they may decide that proper research should be weighted more heavily than eye contact during a presentation.)

11. For long-term tasks, teachers should work with students to draft rubrics.

12. The teacher makes the guidelines available to everyone, whether on a separate handout or as a display in a conspicuous part of the classroom.

Once the negotiation is completed, the work can begin. Of course, some lessons may not lend themselves as readily to negotiated assessment, and some do not require formal assessment at all.

To subscribe to negotiable contracting is to embrace coaching, for both strategies are based on trust, on rapport, and on the permission to work together that both the teacher and the students give one another, acknowledging that it is essential for success.

The Wave Formula

During regular assessment, teachers must decide whether students are to be assessed individually, in pairs, in groups, or as a whole class. During coached assessment, however, the teacher's role is more fluid, like a wave rolling across the sea. First, the teacher-coach works with the classroom as a whole, negotiating the criteria for the assignment. Then the focus narrows: If students are working in groups, the teacher scans the groups for signs of problems, attending to those that are having trouble before moving on to the others. The teacher's focus then narrows even more to deal with individual students who might need nurturing or added clarification. Throughout, the coach's role is to determine whether students are pulling their weight and supporting one another.

These shifts in focus meet the needs of the differentiated classroom. Once the teacher-coach has assisted individual students, his focus zooms out again to scan the groups, and then pulls back further to scan the classroom as a whole. After completing this wave of scans (see Figure 4.1), the coach may tell the class that modifications to the initial contract of assessment criteria are needed.

Life Sciences Secondary School teacher Lydia Caprarella found the wave formula particularly useful. "I am able to observe the class as a whole and troubleshoot," she noted. "As I begin to adjust my proximity and height level to groups that need assistance, I can more readily be on their level to see what their individual or collective concerns are, what their papers say, and so on. Also, by adjusting my stature, I am not the all-seeing, all-knowing teacher; I am someone who can offer guidance without intimidation. I can then pull back or 'crest' again to watch for more problems."

The wave formula is not chiseled in stone; teacher-coaches will find that it will be modified on countless occasions. For example, if a student comes up and asks a question that needs immediate attention, a good coach would address the issue immediately.

The following is an example of modified coached assessment.

• • •

Ms. Price's middle school class was creating and charting colonial settlement sites on contour maps. Each group in the class was to create a site for

The Wave Formula

The steps of the coached assessment wave are as follows:

1. Engaging the whole class
2. Scanning/helping cooperative groups
3. Scanning/helping individual students

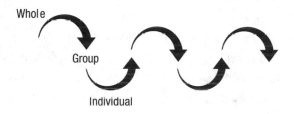

one of the following: the Dutch, the French, the English, the Spanish, the Quakers, the Puritans, and the Huguenots. The assessment criteria, which had already been charted, were as follows:

- The settlement design depicts the needs of the settlers.
- Everything is drawn to scale.
- Placement of settlements makes sense in relation to the contour lines and geographical landmarks on the maps.
- All items are colored realistically. [This item was added by Ms. Price.]

Midway through the project, Ms. Price suddenly noticed that some of the groups were actually using contour lines to delineate fields and distinct patches of earth, forgetting that the lines were to be invisible demarcations representing shifts in ground elevation. So, Ms. Price brought the class together and said that further explanation was needed. After clarifying the intended purpose of contour lines, she reexamined the criteria for assessment along with the students. The criterion stating that all items were to be colored realistically had to be renegotiated; the new criterion read, "Items *and map* are colored realistically." Ms. Price coached the students accordingly.

• • •

By bringing further clarification in the previous example, Ms. Price shifted responsibility to the students by modifying the assessment criteria, which became an essential aid to their self-evaluation. She was able to coach the students unobtrusively to alleviate a roadblock and get the project progressing correctly by first working with the groups to assess their instructional needs.

Unless teacher-coaches provide students with feedback at suitable intervals while they're working, the quality of their completed assignments will be beneath teachers' expectations. According to Goldsmith (1997), business managers who rely solely on employee progress reports to modify their behavior improve by about 46 to 48 percent. By contrast, those who actually follow up on their reports by consulting with employees and responding to their concerns see their scores improve by as much as 95 percent. Some teacher-coaches attest to similar findings: When they work the classroom as coaches on a constant basis, roaming from group to group, following up and responding to the needs and comments of their students, they see the quality of work improve.

Problem Solving 5

Essential Question: How can problem solving play a part in the classroom environment?

Guiding Questions and Statements:
- Describe in detail the components of an effective goal.
- Explain in detail the different models of problem solving that can be used in the classroom.
- Describe specific strategies that promote a problem-solving environment.
- In what ways can the classroom reflect on best practices?
- For what reasons can best practices help solve current problems or complete tasks at hand?

• • •

In this chapter, we examine how to design lessons and projects, how teachers can help students meet goals and establish their own objectives, and what teachers can do when students are confronted with a personal problem.

SMART Goals

When designing lessons for students, it's important to consider whether or not the goal that you pose is specific, measurable, achievable, realistic, and time-oriented—in a word, SMART. We've borrowed the "SMART" acronym from the corporate world. Let's examine each element in detail.

S = Specific. Has the teacher clearly described the goal, so that students understand what is expected of them? At the administrative level, does the superintendent work with principals to set clear, specific goals?

M = Measurable. Can you clearly observe a difference between the point at which the goal was set and the point at which it was finally achieved?

A = Achievable. Is the goal both challenging and reachable, given the students' prior knowledge?

R = Realistic. Are students able to achieve the goal given their other responsibilities, such as homework for other classes and extracurricular activities?

T = Time-Oriented. Can the goal be achieved in a timely manner? Are the expectations clear as to when the goal is to be achieved?

Case Study of a SMART Assignment

The following case study provides an example of an assignment that meets the SMART criteria.

• • •

Ms. Price knew that teaching her social studies class all about North American colonial settlements would be no picnic, but she was determined to succeed. The class was a mixed bag: Quite a few of the students were reading below grade level, and a few had serious problems with absenteeism. Over half the students came from immigrant backgrounds.

The day's activity was a group reading of *Eating the Plates,* Lucille Recht Penner's graphic retelling of the Pilgrims' voyage to the New World. Ms. Price found that although many of the difficult vocabulary words had to be explained, her students were interested in the story. They found it hard to believe that a three-month voyage across the ocean could be so miserable and difficult.

Ms. Price combined the reading with a project in which students took on the role of early immigrants making their journey to a specific colony. The students were to bring to school everything that they planned to bring with them to the colonial settlements, but only what they could carry in a valise.

When the students arrived in class with their "immigrant" luggage, Ms. Price announced that they were going to simulate what it would be like to make a settlement in North America.

"The time period is the 1600s," she said. "Working in your cooperative groups, you must all decide which nationality, religious sect, or stock company you represent on your voyage. [She had to explain the terms 'religious sect' and 'stock company.'] You must work together and decide how to build your settlement, and you must agree on everything you'll need to survive in the wilderness. You have six days to research and design your settlement."

When Ms. Price informed the class that they were to create bird's-eye views of their settlements, she was inundated by questions (and a lot of moaning). She modeled the task for the class, first slicing an apple and asking the students how each layer could be represented on a piece of paper. To familiarize the students with the use of the maps, Ms. Price gave each group pieces of sliced foam, explaining that their configurations represented distinct landforms. Ms. Price went from group to group, observing the students determine how every layer of foam designated a different elevation. Eventually, everyone in the class understood what all of the squiggly lines on the map meant. Each group, working with its own set of foam, was able to draw a contour of the landform after assembling the pieces. The hands-on activity enabled the students to see the highs and the lows that the lines on the contour map represented, and it allowed them to decide how they would want to make use of the land.

Next, Ms. Price told the students that they would have a selection of sites to choose from. When the students saw that it was a pre-prepared contour map on a 30- by 36-inch sheet of blueprint, they were delighted. In four of the blueprints, there were small bodies of water—either the shoreline of an ocean or the banks of a river or lake—in each corner. Two other blueprints had rivers running diagonally across them.

Ms. Price asked the class, "For what reasons do you think the water was so important?"

Lashawn Williams was quick to answer. "That's where the first immigrants stepped ashore," she said.

Maylee Chou also answered correctly: "There were only narrow Indian trails in the woods, so the Europeans used the water to travel and to communicate with each other."

To help out her class as much as possible without actually doing the work herself, Ms. Price gave each group a sample set of illustrations of objects necessary for building a colonial settlement, all drawn from a bird's-eye view. Mr. Fenner, the school's math teacher, worked with Ms. Price over several days on an activity for helping students understand scale. It was a fun, hands-on lesson: Each student chose a cartoon character from a large selection provided by the teacher, then drew the figure in an enlarged scale of 1:4. The students knew that one fourth of an inch on their contour maps equaled 16 feet in real life, and thus were able to apply this understanding of ratios to enlarging the cartoons.

• • •

In the above case study, Ms. Price had put her SMART strategy in place. The goals for the settlement project were

• **Specific.** Students were to design a colonial site plan.
• **Measurable.** Students had to research and write reports and plan a settlement design.
• **Achievable.** Students had the prior knowledge necessary to complete their projects, and the relevant books in the classroom workstation reflected students' reading levels.
• **Realistic.** The class was divided into groups of four; group members divided up the tasks among themselves and supported one another's efforts.
• **Time-Oriented.** Students worked on the project for a full week in class and were given the opportunity to work at home.

The GOPER Model

The coaching process can be broken down into five stages for class, group, or individual work. Teacher-coaches should help students to

G = Focus on the *goal.*
O = Understand their *options.*
P = Create and implement a *plan.*
E = *Eliminate* roadblocks.
R = *Reflect* on what they accomplish.

Let's examine how Ms. Price follows the five steps of the GOPER Model in assisting her student groups.

GOPER Stage 1: Focusing on the Goal

The art of teacher-coaching lies in bringing awareness to students and focusing their attention. By using the questions and comments below, teachers can help their students figure out what they want to accomplish, rather than simply telling them what to do. When students figure out their goals for themselves, they feel a sense of ownership.

We recommend that teachers start by asking general questions and then hone in on more specific ones. The more information students uncover by themselves, the more attention they will pay to the task.

- "Describe your goal in detail."
- "What would you like to focus on today?"
- "What specifically are you planning to accomplish?"
- "Now that you know the situation, explain in detail what you will to do to change it."
- "Now that you understand what we are about to investigate, what specifically bothers you the most? What obstacles might you encounter?"
- "Describe what you need to do. What choices are of interest to your group?"
- "What problem that you want to focus on solving affects you the most?"
- "In what ways will your goal meet the expectations of the assignment?"
- "How can you help the members of your group focus on the work at hand?"
- "What do you most urgently want to change?"

The most effective goals are those that all members of a group can clearly understand. The more specific and targeted the goals are, the more the group can comprehend them. It is essential for the group to agree on the goals and to list them, as an informal contract to support one another. The teacher-coach may use the list as an assessment while circulating the classroom. By using the wave formula as described in Chapter 4, the coach observes whether students are working in harmony and can communicate their goals.

Let's return to Ms. Price's interactions with Lashawn's group. The following vignette shows how Ms. Price helps the group to focus on the goal.

• • •

Ms. Price approaches Lashawn's group and uses the 3 Ps + C Model to help them arrive at their goal.

Ms. Price: May I join you for a few minutes [*permission*]? I would like to hear about your site plan project [*purpose*]. I know you all have the necessary abilities and that you can be creative. I'm sure that you can make your colonial site a success, as you've done on previous projects [*positive suggestion/support*].

Lashawn: I think we'll do okay. So far we work well together.

Ms. Price: What is the most important thing you have to determine before starting this project [*clarity*]?

Timmy: We have to decide what group we want to be. We also have to decide where to build our colonial site.

Pablo: We all have some ideas, but at this point we can't agree.

Ms. Price: What might be beneath the lack of agreement?

Tina: We don't have much specific information, but we've done the assigned readings. I guess we haven't shared enough with each other.

Ms. Price: I saw all the preparatory work that you've done, and I was pleased to see everyone working together. I also liked that everyone took notes as they did their readings from the workstation. You're making headway and moving in the right direction [*compliment*]. What choices are of interest to this group?

Timmy: We don't know enough to make a choice.

Lashawn: I liked the idea of doing a Quaker settlement.

Ms. Price: Tell us a bit more about why you would like to do a Quaker settlement [*purpose*]. What is special about the Quakers that make them different from other colonial groups [*clarity*]?

Lashawn: They helped runaway slaves.

Tina: We all read about Harriet Tubman and the Underground Railroad last year. The Amish left their country, just as my family left China.

Ms. Price: Describe in detail what sets them apart from other colonists and communities in America [*discussion/research questions*].

Lashawn: Quakers are like the Amish that live in the Pennsylvania Dutch country.

Timmy: Yeah, like in the movie *Witness* with Harrison Ford.

Pablo: It was on TV last week. The barn-raising scene was great!

Timmy: They're cool. They don't fight, and they don't make war. They're against killing.

Pablo: Since my family came from Colombia, I guess it would be interesting to learn about others who came to the United States. People from our church really helped us. It's just like the Amish working together to build the barn.

Timmy: All that my family knows is St. Patrick's Day on March 17. I really liked how the boy rang the bell to get his community together to come for help at the end of the movie. It reminds me of my dad at the fire station. Okay, I'll go along with the Quakers.

Ms. Price: This is not an easy task, but I like how you are discussing it together [*reinforcing positive behaviors*]. I like to see you cooperating, and all contributing [*compliment*]. What will you need to do?

Tina: We'll have to read about the Quakers. We can use some of the books at the workstation.

Ms. Price: Your written reports together with the site plan will really result in an excellent project. What would you like to focus on that you think is very important for making your site plan [*focusing on the goal*]?

Timmy: We know the Quakers were a religious group.

Pablo: They probably got chased out of where they lived because of their religion.

Lashawn: We would have to show that their religion was an important part of their lives.

Tina: Our site wouldn't need a fort, like others. The Quakers were a peaceful people, and they got along with the Indians.

Mrs. Price: I'll be checking in with you a bit later to see how you are coming along [*support*].

Just as Lashawn, Tina, Timmy, and Pablo all settled on making a Quaker settlement as their site plan, other groups discussed their own options and made similar decisions: Dylan's group decided to create a settlement similar to Jamestown, Virginia; Maylee's group chose to be Puritans, settling near Boston; James's group picked the Dutch, who settled in Manhattan and along the Hudson River; Darlene's group chose to be religious dissenters fleeing the Puritans and settling in Connecticut. Other groups decided to build settlements based on those of the Swedes, Spaniards, Scotch-Irish, and French.

GOPER Stage 2: Understanding the Options

Teacher-coaches need to let groups determine their options for themselves, rather than impose a course of action on them. Ownership is paramount here: When a group falters, the coach should guide students to a better understanding of available options, rather than simply taking over. Once the students have exhausted their own list of options, the teacher can ask them if she may offer some additional help. Teachers can use the following statements and questions to guide students while also ensuring that they retain a sense of ownership:

- "Think about everything you could need or use in order to help you."
- "In what ways will others respond to each of your choices during the discussion?"
- "That's one option, what's another?"
- "Generate a list of the resources you will need to make your position believable."
- "Where could you get other books and resources?"
- "Let me know what you uncover in your research."
- "Some of these resources you've listed can't be found in the library. Where else do you think you could go to obtain them?"
- "Do you feel comfortable going to the museum, public library, or county court house to obtain the resources you need? Some students feel comfortable going alone. What about you?"
- "How could you get to the museum, public library, or county court house? Which mode of public transportation would best work for you? Some students have older family members or friends who help them out."

• "Of the resources that you described, which would be the most effective? You can't choose all of them, so which are your top choices?"

• "What steps in this assignment have you experienced previously? How did you manage them?"

The following vignette shows how Ms. Price helped her students to understand their options.

• • •

Ms. Price: Describe how the materials at the workstation helped you with your site plans.

Tina: Some of the books at the workstation are difficult to read.

Ms. Price: Okay, then we'll work on finding books that are more suitable. I'm still glad that you are making the effort. I'm pleased that everyone is trying to get good information for your project [*compliment*]. Where could you get other books that might be easier to handle?

Timmy: I'll check my neighborhood library, but those books are sometimes just as hard.

Tina: A lot of the books at the library aren't specifically about Quakers, and it isn't easy getting the information that we'll need.

Ms. Price: What can you do to make your work and your reading less difficult?

Lashawn: Timmy can bring in the books from the library, and I'll check out the Internet tonight. We can bring in all the books and stuff that we can find and look through them together.

Tina: If they have lots of pictures, that would help and make things easier.

Ms. Price: You're all doing a terrific job in getting information, and your colonial site plan will reflect all of the work you're doing [*compliment*]. May I offer a suggestion [*permission*]? Right here in lower Manhattan there's an organization called the Society of Friends, which is another name for the Quakers. How would you feel about going there?

Tina: I've got stuff to do after school, but I'll really make an effort to look through your workstation during lunch.

Pablo: I have to help my Mom at work when I get home from school, but maybe I could borrow one of the books from Ms. Price.

Ms. Price: If you make the effort to find easier books, I'll look around as well. Okay, so Timmy will be off to the library, Lashawn will check out the Internet, Tina will spend extra time during lunch at the workstation, and Pablo will borrow a book of his choice overnight from the workstation [*positive suggestions/support*]. Is everybody in agreement?
Students: [All nod their heads.]

Ms. Price was concerned with ensuring that all of the groups did the best research they could, using both the workstation and whatever resources they could obtain beyond the school. Though reading might be a problem, Ms. Price was close at hand to guide the students in the classroom. She decided to revisit the library and search the Internet for additional lower-level reading materials.

GOPER Stage 3: Creating and Implementing a Plan

When students list their tasks in order of importance, they can visualize a reasonable plan. Having a plan helps decrease students' anxiety levels, because it allows them to work within a logical framework. Here are some questions and statements that teachers may use to coach students through the prioritizing stage:

- "Describe in detail what your group needs to do."
- "In what ways will your actions help you to prepare properly for the project?"
- "Create a plan of action that will help you achieve your goals. First, write down all the things that you need to do. Once you have your list, place the items in logical order for completion. Now that you have a plan, each one of you will have to take on responsibility in an equitable manner."
- "What is your time line? What comes next? How can you work out a plan?"
- "What does each of you have to do in order to meet your goal?"
- "What roles will you assign to each person so that the task will be completed?"
- "What materials do you need or have? Describe the materials at the workstation that are suitable."
- "How will this help you meet your goal?"

- "Who, if anyone, do you need to contact for support?"
- "Have you shared your telephone numbers or e-mail addresses with each other so that you can support one another? If you need to get together outside of school, have you discussed your schedules?"
- "How can I help and support you?"

It is important to understand that the coach's responsibility is not to resolve the problems that students encounter, but rather to guide students through their questions in a way that encourages them to solve the problems on their own.

Returning to Ms. Price's class, let's see how she helps her students to create and implement a plan of action.

• • •

Ms. Price stayed close to the groups and monitored their activities over the next few days. She was especially anxious about how Lashawn, Tina, Timmy, and Pablo were pursuing their research.

Ms. Price: I see you've brought in some new books, and that you found the materials that were added to the workstation. I'm glad to see you all have your heads together, and that you're carefully discussing all your information [*compliment*].

Timmy: We have lots of information, but we don't know how we want to use it.

Lashawn: We found some pictures that showed early Quaker settlements. That helped us at times more than any of the reading.

Ms. Price: You made a good start gathering information. So, what comes next [*compliment/purpose*]?

Pablo: Everyone wants to write a report on farming because that's what most of the information we found was about.

Timmy: There was other stuff, mostly about religion.

Pablo: But none of us found it interesting.

Tina: That's not true. I think the Quakers' religion was cool. They didn't have priests. There were no rituals and ceremonies. If anyone did something wrong, they stood up at the meeting house and said so to the whole community.

Ms. Price: How can you work out a plan that lets you know who will be writing the research sections?

Lashawn: Well, Tina likes the religion, so if she wants to write a report on that, I have no problem.

Timmy: Anybody interested in their daily life?

Pablo: That's fine by me, as long as I don't have to do the religion.

Ms. Price: I like the way you're communicating [*compliment*]. How can we be sure that all roles are equal [*awareness of others*]?

Timmy: Maybe we should look at the farming section and divide that between two people.

Ms. Price: That's a good idea. If a section is too large, divide it up and share the work equally. As you go along, you'll be able to figure it out [*ownership*].

The next time Ms. Price checked on the group, Lashawn, Tina, Timmy, and Pablo had listed everything that had to be done.

Lashawn: We're all sharing the work.

Ms. Price: Now that you know all of the material, how can you create a reliable design for your site plan of a Quaker settlement [*purpose*]?

Tina: We have two days. That gives us enough time to work together.

Timmy: We're doing some of our own drawings, and everything is being measured out to scale like we did in Mr. Fenner's class.

Pablo: We're using some of the pictures we found in the books.

Timmy: And what we read about the Quakers.

Ms. Price: How will this help you meet your goal? Please give me some examples of how you're designing your site plan [*clarity*].

Lashawn: We know how they farmed, and what crops they planted in their fields.

Pablo: We know how they built their houses, and we have an idea where to put them.

Tina: We should make the meeting house the center of the settlement.

Timmy: We also found that the Quakers knew something about sickness and keeping healthy.

Tina: And we know how to read the map, so we know where it's high and where it's low. Therefore, we know where to dig a well to get fresh water.

Halfway through the class period, Ms. Price approached the group once more as the students were getting ready to put the site together.

Ms. Price: What materials do you need or have, and who is in charge of each task [*purpose*]?

Tina: We all took scissors from the bin, and we're helping Timmy with the cutting.

Timmy: We all have glue sticks, and we're going to help Lashawn with the gluing.

Pablo: We've all got our own markers, and we're going to work with Tina to color the site.

Ms. Price: Let me know how I can help and support you [*positive suggestion/support*].

Because the students in Lashawn's group formulated a plan of action and stuck to it, they were able to successfully complete their assignment. The students all did their readings to the best of their abilities. For the most part, all four students cooperated, sharing the work equally. There were a few instances of petty squabbling, but the students were able to avoid the kinds of major disagreements that sidetracked other groups.

GOPER Stage 4: Eliminating the Roadblocks

Teacher-coaches should first help students probe for obstacles that may not be obvious to the youngsters. Then they should ask the students for permission to share certain views with them. At this point, coaches can point to certain obstacles and ask the students to think about ways to prepare for them, using statements and questions such as the following:

- "What roadblocks do you expect? What questions might you have? What challenges are you experiencing?"
- "Explain in detail what you will need to do to avoid this roadblock. What specifically is stopping you from doing your work?"
- "What issues need to be discussed?"
- "What could be a way around this roadblock?"
- "Place yourself in someone else's shoes, and try to solve the challenge from her perspective."
- "Who could help you avoid this roadblock?"

- "Describe in detail what action you took, and what the effect was. Were any of your actions met with a negative response? If so, which ones, and how did you overcome the negative response?"

- "When asking for help, be polite and make sure to be clear about wanting to actually solve the problem yourself—do not ask anyone to solve it for you."

- "When asking for help from a museum or library, make an appointment and present yourself. There is nothing like a personal appearance when you want help."

- "What needs to be discussed and brought out in the open? What is keeping you from wanting to be involved right now?"

The teacher-coach needs to be objective and make certain that prejudicial attitudes or judgmental opinions never come into play during the give-and-take with students. Phrasing such as, "Why on earth did you do that?" is both provocative and harsh, and can make students embarrassed and defensive. Instead, coaches should use phrasing such as, "I'm curious, what led you to make that decision?" or "What can we learn from this?" It is a rule of thumb that the teacher-coach should use as little evaluative language as possible.

The following vignette from Ms. Price's class shows her helping Lashawn's group to eliminate roadblocks.

• • •

Ms. Price noticed that Timmy was not a happy camper; his chair was turned away, and he was slouching and hanging his head. Ms. Price noticed that Timmy's peers were ignoring him.

Ms. Price: Can I join in for a little while, and see what the group is working on [*permission*]? I'm sensing a disconnect here. What is keeping Timmy from wanting to be involved right now [*hidden/heightened emotions*]?
Lashawn: We're trying to find a location for the Quaker meeting house.
Ms. Price: What challenges are you experiencing [*hidden/heightened emotions*]?
Tina: Timmy keeps insisting it should be a building with a steeple.
Pablo: He wants to put a big church smack in the middle of the settlement.
Timmy: Well, the Quakers were an important religious group, weren't they?

Pablo: We're trying to tell him that Quakers didn't have a church.

Lashawn: Right. They had a meeting house, which is a different kind of building.

Timmy: But why can't it have a steeple, like any church? I thought they were Christians.

Ms. Price: Who can help Timmy understand why his idea for a Quaker meeting house with a steeple might be inappropriate for your settlement [*positive suggestion/support*]?

Tina: The Quakers were different from Catholics and other Christian groups.

Lashawn: They didn't build fancy places to hold religious services or ceremonies.

Pablo: They were simple in how they worshipped.

Tina: And the place where they met was plain.

Lashawn: The meeting house was just a building like any other, only a bit larger to hold all of the people in their community.

Ms. Price: Tell me what kinds of religious buildings that you've seen other than Christian churches. How would you describe the buildings in comparison to a Catholic church?

Pablo: Mohamed lives upstairs from us and he goes to the mosque on 96th Street. It's a plain building from the outside.

Tina: There's a little synagogue on my block, on Hester Street. It looks like any other building except that it has Hebrew writing and the Star of David on the front.

Timmy: OK, OK—make it a plain building. But I still think a church should be something special.

Ms. Price: If I heard Pablo and Tina correctly, Timmy, Quakers were simple people and they did not like anything fancy, similar to other religious groups here in Manhattan [*clarity*]. If that's settled, I think you can move on. I am very pleased with your progress [*compliment*].

GOPER Stage 5: Reflecting

In the last GOPER stage, students think about and reflect on what they've accomplished so they can move forward, or even repeat the process again. The teacher-coach poses open-ended questions that urge students to reply with detailed descriptions. The goal of this stage is to encourage students to become more self-aware by comparing their levels of development before and after the activity. Coaches can use questions and statements such as the following:

- "How well do you think you accomplished what you set out to do? How did you do against your action plan?"
- "For what reasons did you complete what was expected?"
- "Describe in detail what you learned."
- "In reflection, what do you need to add to your plan that you didn't originally consider? A plan that is worked from beginning to end without modification is too rigid. In what ways do you want to change your plan to meet your expectations more effectively?"
- "Tell me about how well you worked together."
- "What could you do to work more efficiently?"
- "How well did you stay on schedule? What precisely did you have to do to meet the time limit? How comfortable are you with how much has been accomplished?"
- "How clear are you about what you need to prepare before your group meets next time? What do you need to do the next time you meet?"
- "Rate your comfort level on today's practice run from 1 to 10. How ready are you for the forum tomorrow?"
- "At what point did you feel that you needed more support?"

Golfing offers an excellent example of effective reflection. Let's say that a gym teacher takes a student out for some practice swings. If the student drives a shot from inside a sand bunker and misses the green, the coach has three options. The first option would be to respond negatively: "You are way off the mark, but you just can't expect to win them all." This would be of no help to the student. The second option is a positively worded response that offers some insight and hints at a possible solution: "It appears that the slope is much steeper than you expected, and the wind is now blowing in your direction." A third option is for the coach to respond with a question of his own that encourages reflection: "Golf is a very difficult and demanding sport. It requires patience, proficiency, and planning. Having said that, what could you have taken into consideration differently?"

Let's return to Ms. Price's class and see how she coaches the students in Lashawn's group to reflect on their accomplishments.

• • •

The next day, when the students had finished their work, Ms. Price approached Lashawn's group.

Ms. Price: I liked the way you pulled together when the need arose. I also like how you overcame your difficulties [*compliment*]. How well do you think you accomplished what you set out to do [*reflection question*]?

Lashawn: I thought we had a good plan to follow.

Timmy: We picked the topic of the Quakers that we were all interested in doing.

Tina: The hardest part was deciding on the cutouts, and where to put everything.

Lashawn: Yeah, but we cooperated and agreed. We only argued a bit.

Timmy: It was good that we all shared the jobs and the work. It made it a lot easier.

Pablo: I found the coloring boring.

Timmy: Yeah. Too much time coloring every part of the contour map.

Lashawn: But look how nice it looks. It makes the Quaker settlement look real with all the beautiful colors.

Ms. Price: So, you felt that you worked well together and you like the end result, but coloring the site plan was a bit too much. At what point did you feel that you needed more support [*reflection question*]?

Lashawn: I found that some of the books were difficult.

Pablo: But the books you brought after we talked were very helpful.

Tina: The pictures of early Quaker settlements in some of the books also helped.

Ms. Price: How well did you stay on schedule [*reflection question*]?

Tina: I thought we completed everything on time.

Pablo: Especially after we finished doing the reading and writing our reports.

Lashawn: We probably wasted more time arguing about whether a Quaker meeting house should have a steeple.

Pablo: After talking about it, we finally decided it should be a plain building, just much larger than all the rest.

Ms. Price: It was a challenge making a compromise, but your group certainly pulled together [*compliment*].

At the end of the activity, each group gave an oral presentation explaining how it created its settlement, and upon what information it based its construction. Each group spoke for a few minutes, explaining what made its colonial settlement different from the others in North America. After each presentation, the group answered questions from the class.

For Ms. Price and her entire class, the site-planning lesson was a challenging and enjoyable learning experience. All of the groups encountered more or less the same problems as Lashawn, Tina, Timmy, and Pablo— minor pitfalls that they always confronted and gradually surmounted, and that sometimes even propelled them forward. By having the groups create nine separate settlement plans, with an oral presentation and Q&A session for each, Ms. Price enabled her students to gain a truly comprehensive overview of "the Peopling of America."

Teacher-coaches can use the GOPER Model with individuals as well as with groups. "I implemented the GOPER Model with one of my students," said Jeff Hopper, a teacher at Alice E. Grady Elementary School in Elmsford, New York. "It helped her focus and understand, and I think we came up with a good plan of action."

Many students who have been trained in coaching find the strategy helpful. "While using the GOPER Model, I noticed that this approach relieves all the confusion and the hassle," said Romaine Hall, a 10th grader at Life Sciences Secondary School. "I was able to focus."

GOPER Assessment Form

Teacher-coaches can use the form in Figure 5.1 to assess group progress at each GOPER stage. The form also serves as a reminder for teachers to revisit specific groups and follow up on issues of concern. Teachers can modify the form for use with different types of assignments.

The 3-Step Reflective Process

There are always moments when students hit a wall and are suddenly confronted by a problem that seems impossible to solve. In such situations,

Figure 5.1

GOPER Assessment Form

Names of Students, Team Name, or Table Number:

Topic:

G: Has the group established its goal(s)? What is the goal or are the students still brainstorming?

Date:

Date:

O: In what ways do the students have a good comprehension of their options?

Date:

Date:

P: Describe in detail the group's plan of action:

Date:

Date:

E: Does the group have any roadblocks? If so, describe specifically how the students are handling them:

Date:

Date:

R: Explain whether or not the group members examine and reflect upon their actions as they move along. In what ways did they learn from working with one another or from accomplishing this project or task?

Date:

Date:

Dates Completed:	**Goal**	**Options**	**Plan of Action**	**Eliminate the Roadblocks**	**Reflection**

Comments and Reminders:

Date:

Date:

teacher-coaches can come to the rescue with the 3-Step Reflective Process. During this process, the coach works with the student to reflect upon similar instances in the past, determine what course of action was successful then and why, and consider how to apply a similar solution to the current problem.

Teachers can use the following questions and statements to guide students through the three steps:

Step 1
- "What in the past was similar to what you are dealing with currently?"
- "How were you able to solve the problem then?"
- "Describe what allowed you to succeed."

Step 2
- "Why did the solution work so well previously?"
- "How can you assess what worked?"
- "Describe what specific steps you took."

Step 3
- "How can you apply your prior knowledge to the current situation?"
- "What powerful information from your previous experience can be applied now?"
- "What strengths and resources do you have that will help you achieve your current goal?"

Case Study of the 3-Step Reflective Process

To see how the 3-Step Reflective Process works, let's travel to Mrs. Orlov's science classroom.

• • •

Mrs. Orlov has noticed that Basja, usually an actively involved student, is focusing her attention beyond the classroom window. Though she occasionally brings her attention back to the class, overall she appears unfocused and disinterested.

Mrs. Orlov: Basja, you were assigned to read the section on how hydroelectric power is generated, but it appears that you are focused elsewhere.

Basja: I didn't understand the textbook. I get frustrated when there aren't any pictures or diagrams.

Mrs. Orlov: Could it be because you're a visual learner?

Basja: Well, I don't know about that, but art is my favorite subject.

Mrs. Orlov: Fine, Basja. You're an artist and have a special talent. In your other classes, when you don't understand the text, what do you do to help yourself? *(Step 1)*

Basja: Well, in math class, I like to use those fun materials—the canisters—for algebra.

Mrs. Orlov: Explain; tell me why that helps you.

Basja: Because I pretend that the *x* is hidden inside the canister. I can see what the algebraic expression means.

Mrs. Orlov: Once you no longer have the need to use the cans, how do you finish your class work and complete your homework assignments? *(Step 2)*

Basja: I draw them in my notebook. After a while, I don't need the drawings, but they help me out in the beginning to understand what I'm doing.

Mrs. Orlov: How could you apply your special artistic talent here, in science class? *(Step 3)*

Basja: I haven't given it much thought, but I could try to draw a picture as I read each section in the text.

Mrs. Orlov: That's a great idea, and I think it will work.

Basja: But what do I do if I get confused and stuck?

Mrs. Orlov: Don't worry, Basja. I'll keep an eye on you as I oversee the class. If I see that you're having difficulties, I'll come over and help. If you're pleased with your drawings when you're finished, do you think we could use them as a model for the class to help the others understand hydroelectric power?

•   •   •

Students at Life Sciences Secondary School who have been trained to use coaching found the 3-Step Reflective Process helpful. "It allows for a degree of progressivism in the individual," said Darling Jimenez, "since one records past trials and utilizes the lessons learned to solve new and similar problems."

6 Individual Coaching

Essential Questions:
- What is individual coaching?
- In what ways does individual coaching affect classroom practices?

Guiding Questions and Statements:
- Describe in detail the steps of one-on-one coaching.
- In what ways does the knowledge of multiple viewpoints add perspective to a problem?
- How do gremlins, assumptions, interpretations, and limiting beliefs hinder productivity?

• • •

When a group's difficulties center on one particular student, there are times when the teacher-coach's gut feeling is to personally intervene. In these instances, the best step to take may be to pull the student aside for a personalized coaching session. If a few minutes of discussion suffice, then nothing further may need to be said; however, sometimes further intervention is necessary.

The teacher-coach should schedule any initial one-on-one discussion with a student to occur during study hall or the lunch period, or after school. It is most important that the teacher not compromise the student's standing in class, and even more imperative to develop a feeling of mutual trust with her; for these reasons, the student should not be placed in an embarrassing predicament.

The Six Steps of Individual Coaching

The six major steps of individual coaching are as follows:

1. Requesting to meet
2. Discovery
3. Designing an action plan
4. Developing tools of growth
5. Monitoring
6. Letting go

A classroom example follows the description of each step in the sections below.

Step 1: Requesting to Meet

During the initial one-on-one meeting, the teacher-coach must clearly and precisely list the behaviors he's seen the student engage in. He must explain to the student that, though she has some very good attributes, she is engaging in behaviors that concern him. The job of the coach is to elicit more positive behaviors through one-on-one dialogues.

The teacher-coach should explain that they will focus on the student's needs. They should agree on a regular meeting place and on a time that suits their schedules. Then, the coach and student need to reach some sort of agreement and create an atmosphere of trust that will enable them to work together. Negotiated agendas can only work if the student feels that the teacher wholeheartedly cares about her, and if she is confident in the coaching process. What better way is there to gain the student's confidence than by asking the student's permission to continue working together?

Let's walk through this step with Mr. Connelly, who is using individual coaching with his student Vicky, from his 10th grade science class.

• • •

The members of Vicky's group approached Mr. Connelly to tell him that they did not want her in the group anymore. Though she was cute and had a vibrant personality, she was also totally unreliable: Whenever she brought in homework for a group project, it was crinkled, stained with food, missing parts, incomprehensible, and invariably late. Other group members often did Vicky's work for her, fearing that her efforts would lower their grades. No matter how much Vicky said she wanted to help, she was never successful.

After Mr. Connelly met with the others in Vicky's group to get a pulse of the situation, he decided to make a pro/con T-chart to help guide his thinking (see Figure 6.1).

Figure 6.1
Mr. Connelly's Initial Pro/Con T-Chart for Vicky

Pro	Con
Fun	Unreliable
Cute/attractive	Poor physical shape of homework
Vibrant personality	Illegible/messy writing
Good company	Late

After completing his chart, Mr. Connelly met with Vicky. He highlighted the fact that all of her classmates considered her a terrific person—everyone liked her company and warm personality. However, members of the group had requested that she be assigned elsewhere because they felt they could not rely on her to get the work done.

Mr. Connelly asked Vicky if she would consider meeting with him, twice a week at a mutually convenient time, so that he could offer some help. He pointed out that someone with so many good qualities could surely make things better, and that he might even be able to offer her some tools for doing so. Vicky agreed to meet every Tuesday and Friday for 10 minutes at the beginning of 6th period, when neither of them had class.

Step 2: Discovery

Finding out the student's personal beliefs and attitudes toward education is most important. Teacher-coaches can use the following questions and statements to uncover such information:

- "How does your family show interest in your education?"
- "How do you believe education will influence your career when you grow up?"
- "How does your home environment contribute to or counter your ability to do homework?"
- "What do you value the most when working with other students in your group?"
- "When do you feel that you have the greatest success?"
- "When do you feel that you are not successful?"
- "Explain specifically what happens to you when you get stuck."
- "How do you handle the pressures of school work?"
- "Describe what you feel when others are disappointed in you."

Of course, the teacher-coach can only be expected to handle responses related to the student's learning. If disturbing personal issues come up at this stage, the coach should advise the student to meet with a school guidance counselor, social worker, or professional therapist.

● ● ●

Mr. Connelly reflected on Vicky's work over the first two months and noticed a pattern. Her homework was invariably late or lost. Her group work was incomplete, poorly written, and even nonexistent at times. Some of Vicky's work was stained by food. Vicky was to supply books and materials to the group on several occasions, but never did.

Mr. Connelly decided to ask Vicky some questions to determine the roots of her difficulties. He found out that she liked school and being in after-school clubs. She especially liked the company of friends. At home, her parents always encouraged her with school work and emphasized to her the importance of education; however, they worked evenings. Vicky's room was always a mess, no matter how often she was reminded to clean it up. She said she constantly lost things—papers and her assignments always ended up in the wrong books and places—and expressed deep remorse for letting her group down when they were counting on her.

After meeting with Vicky, Mr. Connelly modified his initial pro/con T-chart (see Figure 6.2).

Figure 6.2

Mr. Connelly's Modified Pro/Con T-Chart for Vicky

Pro	Con
Fun	Unreliable
Cute/attractive	Poor physical shape of homework
Vibrant personality	Illegible/messy writing
Good company	Late
Gets encouragement from parents about education	Flaky
Likes school	Parents not home after school/evenings
Likes her friends	Room at home is a mess
Has a caring conscience	Always loses things

Step 3: Designing an Action Plan

When helping a student draft a plan of action, the teacher-coach shouldn't burden her with too many items that need to be changed. He should work hand-in-hand with the student to brainstorm a list and ask her to rank the items in order of importance. Even though this is a negotiated process, the student must ultimately take ownership of it. The teacher and the student should then collectively decide on the two or three items that they will work to improve.

Throughout this process, the teacher-coach must be firmly committed to a meaningful, relevant relationship. By asking the student to meet weekly or semiweekly to discuss her progress, the teacher is asking for permission to continue developing the bond of trust and confidence. The teacher and student should mutually decide how much time they want to devote to the plan of action.

• • •

Mr. Connelly asked Vicky to list her specific issues of concern, and to star whichever issues she wanted to work on first. Her list read as follows:

- Keeping my room clean
- Organizing my books
- Finding my homework
- Finding anything: coats, keys, books

- Knowing when assignments are due
- Taking proper notes *
- Organizing notes and making them into a report
- Organizing my time *
- Being punctual
- Getting things ready on time *
- Working at my desk at home

Vicky and Mr. Connelly agreed that they would first tackle the smaller issues that would make her life more manageable. Next, she drafted the following action plan:

Contract

Goal: To become better organized in general

Initial Objectives:

1. To use an organizer
2. To take notes properly
3. To remind myself of important due dates

Mr. Connelly asked Vicky what she could purchase to help her with each of these items. Vicky responded that she could purchase a spiral bound notebook, a set of multicolored highlighters, and a pack of sticky notes for their next meeting.

They agreed to work together on Vicky's plan and assess her development at the end of the term.

Step 4: Developing Tools of Growth

The teacher-coach and student should discuss what tools the student will need to reach the objectives set out in the action plan. Just defining the tools and letting the student determine how to work them is not enough; the coach should also discuss useful strategies.

• • •

Mr. Connelly helped Vicky brainstorm a list of tools and strategies that she could use to accomplish her goals and asked her to star the ones she wanted to work on first. Her list read as follows:

- Learn how to use an organizer*
- Study habits

- ○ Take notes—write a bullet on a sticky note and place it on the paragraph
- ○ Place bolded terms on flash cards, separate into groups by chapters
- Make organizer lists—what is due in a week, in two weeks
- Place reminders on medicine cabinet door or on headboard of bed—somewhere I normally look
- Set phone alarm for a daily reminder
- Hang keys on a key hook routinely (rituals)*
- Monitor different stages of work to make sure it'll be ready when due
- Research—find books on topic; pick up book; scan book for relevant chapter; take notes; write first draft, second draft, and final draft
- Color-code the week—block out class times, activities, scheduling, research, social life
- Make checklists
- Place corkboard by desk at home to pin up bulletins and other items*

Together, Mr. Connelly and Vicky discussed how to use an organizer. Vicky decided to write her assignments in it, choosing her colors purposefully (pink for assignment deadlines, blue for errands, and yellow for appointments). Mr. Connelly asked Vicky how she could use sticky notes to write down important ideas from the text. She responded that she could write the ideas on a sticky note and stick the note on top of the relevant paragraph in the book. Once she reached the end of the chapter, Vicky could take the sticky notes, line them up, and transcribe all the notes into a spiral notebook, where the pages could not be lost. To remind herself of particular pressing assignments, Mr. Connelly asked Vicky to write down the task and its due date on a sticky note, and then place it where she would see it routinely. Vicky chose the medicine cabinet in her bathroom.

After her discussion with Mr. Connelly, Vicky reported that she felt comfortable trying out the new strategies and would give them her best effort.

Step 5: Monitoring

During the monitoring process, the teacher and student discuss what has been working well and what needs tweaking. Because errors bruise us emotionally, we're more likely to remember them; thus, we can often learn more from falling short than from successes. The coach's job is to help students realize that disappointments can be turned into positive lessons.

• • •

Slowly, Vicky began to make progress. At first, Mr. Connelly and Vicky reviewed her organizer and discussed whether or not the sticky notes helped. She said they were easy to use and served as good reminders. It took a few weeks for Vicky to get the hang of using the organizer. She took particular care because she knew that Mr. Connelly wanted her to do well; she also enjoyed the feeling of being a bit more in control of her life.

Vicky purchased a hook on which to hang her house keys when she got home. She placed a corkboard over her desk and posted important notices and dates on it. Though Vicky made an effort to keep her room clean, it was a struggle. She made an agreement with Mr. Connelly that he would only ask how her room was on Tuesdays. They agreed that Vicky should try to clean up her room on Sunday nights.

Soon, Vicky became less prone to losing things. Her school work began to improve; her life was gaining a semblance of organization. It didn't all happen overnight, but then Rome wasn't built in a day.

Step 6: Letting Go

In the beginning, a student may need to be monitored twice a week. Within that limited amount of time, it might be hard to see results. The coach should explain to the student that progress is achieved in little steps, so it may not be immediately noticed, but that the steps accumulate over time to make the goal a reality. Once the student has reached her goals, the teacher-coach should start weaning her from his support. One-on-one meetings should become fewer and farther between, until they are no longer necessary. Once the student is prepared to work confidently and independently at school, the coach lets go of her so she can fly on her own.

GAIL

The inadequacies that many students feel when confronting their work can be ascribed to the effects of GAIL: gremlins, assumptions, interpretations, and limiting beliefs. Students often point to these factors because they don't want to be embarrassed by failure, which may lower their self-esteem. It is the teacher-coach's job to confront GAIL roadblocks and reframe the situation so that students can move forward.

G = Gremlins. As described in Chapter 3, gremlins are the voices in students' psyches that call out, "I just can't do it." In chemistry class, Felix approaches the periodic table as though it were the Rosetta stone: His forehead breaks into beads of heavy perspiration, his heart starts to palpitate rapidly, and he begins to stutter.

A = Assumptions. Assumptions are ideas based on past events. If Ashley had trouble learning algebra in Mr. Heller's class, then she assumes she'll also have trouble with geometry in Ms. Fallow's class—even though Ms. Fallow is a new teacher with new strategies, and geometry is completely different from algebra.

I = Interpretations. Interpretations are our subjective perceptions of events. When Stuart lightly taps Charnel on the shoulder, she turns briskly and forcefully says, "Don't hit me." Stuart, who grew up in a physically competitive home with three brothers, interprets his tap differently than Charnel, who only has a younger sister.

L = Limiting beliefs. Limiting beliefs are ideas about the world that we believe to be unchangeable, even though they are often not based on fact. Hugo's limiting belief is that men are always better athletes than women—even though Romanian gymnast Nadia Comaneci shattered Olympic records in 1976 with perfect scores of 10.

Breakthrough Laser Coaching

Breakthrough Laser Coaching (Institute for Professional Empowerment Coaching, 2005) helps students to "break through" tough situations as they occur, whether inside or outside the classroom. By using a "laser technique," the coaching strategy allows students to fix a problem themselves rather than rely on a teacher-coach to fix it for them. It helps students eliminate self doubts while at the same time establishing teachers as their partners in problem solving. According to Sara DiBenedetto, a teacher at Queens Academy High School in New York City, "It is a good technique because, if successful, you can get a change in behavior from students without having judged them."

Breakthrough Laser Coaching consists of discussing a person's thoughts, feelings, and actions. In Stage 1, the student reflects on the situation that is causing conflict; in Stage 2, the student creates a new self-image that helps to eliminate the conflict. The following case study offers a good example of the strategy in action.

● ● ●

Stephanie McKenzie is 16 years old. She has two brothers, one older and one younger, and grew up playing sports just as they did. Growing up, her father had been on the high school football team, while her mother enjoyed jazz, ballet, and figure skating. Whenever her mother pushed Stephanie toward typically female activities, Stephanie resisted. This pressure gradually made Stephanie angrier and more mean-spirited; by the time she was in high school, she often acted out in class and belittled other girls.

While working in cooperative groups on a project, Stephanie's teacher, Mr. Hall, noticed that some girls in the class avoided working with her, and that Stephanie herself preferred working with the boys. He decided to discuss the matter with Stephanie after school using Breakthrough Laser Coaching. To remember the three initial steps of this strategy, the teacher-coach might attach a physical motion to each one; for example, he could brush back his hair for "thought," tap his hand on his heart for "feeling," and wiggle his hands for "action."

Stage 1: Analysis of the Current Dilemma

Step 1: Thought. Mr. Hall asked Stephanie to please explain why she preferred working with the boys in the class. She said that she enjoyed playing sports with the boys, and she didn't like to fuss about herself as much as the other girls did. Mr. Hall probed further, asking Stephanie how her parents felt about her relationship with boys. She explained that her mother pressured her unduly to be more feminine, trying to get her to wear lace undergarments, make-up, and high heels, but that she preferred to be more natural. She even dreamed of playing on the boys' hockey team, which would surely be received as a betrayal by her mother.

Step 2: Feeling. Mr. Hall asked Stephanie how she felt about her situation. She responded that not being able to be herself made her angry. She simply found more in common with boys and the sports they played than with girls. Because her mother couldn't relate, this created great friction.

Step 3: Action. Mr. Hall said that he noticed Stephanie's resistance to working with other girls, and the inappropriate jokes she would sometimes make about them. He told her that her actions reflected her feelings, and asked her to reflect on other ways in which her mother's pressure made her act unlike her authentic self. Stephanie admitted that she was pushing other girls away, using jokes, snide remarks, and put-downs because she didn't know where to place her anger. She wasn't jealous of the other girls; she just knew she could never be like them—that is, the way her mother always wanted her to be—so she felt defeated.

Step 4: Validation. Mr. Hall told Stephanie that it was understandable that having parents with limiting beliefs could be difficult. It was reasonable to have feelings of anger, and he didn't entirely blame her. He did, however, point out that belittling her female classmates hadn't gotten Stephanie anywhere, and that her social growth appeared to have stalled.

Stage 2: Building a New Image

Step 1: Thought. Mr. Hall asked Stephanie if she would like to work on her issues with other girls so that she could be happier, and she said yes. He told Stephanie that through coaching, she could create a new self-image, leading to new opportunities. Stephanie said that she would like to tell her parents she preferred male-oriented sports, and that she would like to try out for the boys' ice hockey team.

Step 2: Feeling. Mr. Hall asked Stephanie how pursuing her heartfelt goals would make her feel. She said that trying out for the hockey team would be incredible, and that she couldn't resist the notion. She had several posters hanging in her room of Manon Rheaume of the Tampa Bay Lightning—the first female goalie in the National Hockey League. Stephanie pulled out a notebook from her book bag and showed Mr. Hall a picture of Rheaume that she had glued to the cover. She looked at him and said that she hoped her picture would be on the cover of *Sports Illustrated* one day.

Step 3: Action. Mr. Hall asked Stephanie what she could do to make her new self-image a reality. Stephanie said that she would like to make her case to try out for the team to the school's athletic director. Mr. Hall asked her what supporting evidence she could bring with her to strengthen her case. Stephanie replied that not only could she bring in examples of Manon, but she could also do an Internet search and find other women who played professionally in male-dominated sports. She said she would also check to see if there were girls in other nearby high schools playing on boys' teams. Mr. Hall asked her when she could get her supporting evidence ready. Stephanie replied enthusiastically that she'd "hit the Internet" during study hall, as she couldn't wait until she got home.

Mr. Hall asked Stephanie how she could gain support at home for what she wanted to do. Stephanie replied that she couldn't approach her mother by herself. After a moment's silence, she said that she could get all of her research together; show the research to her brothers first, then to her father; and finally sit down as a family together to talk to her mother. Mr. Hall said that for her to take the chance to make her dream come true would be outstanding. He wanted to be realistic with her though, so he reminded her that she might not make the team; still, he said, to not give it a try would be a regret that she would live with forever.

Step 4: Accountability. Mr. Hall reflected on the Breakthrough Laser Coaching session with Stephanie. He asked her if she was comfortable with her plan to do the proper research, talk with her family at different stages, and then approach the athletic director at school. She answered that although she had felt very much alone before their conversation, she now felt as though she had a support system thanks to him. They both left the 20-minute session feeling that Stephanie might be able to channel her energies more appropriately, so that her authentic self could emerge.

The Administrator's Role 7

Essential Question: What does a coaching school look like?

Guiding Questions and Statements:
 • Specifically describe the principal's role in coaching an assistant principal.
 • Explain in detail how a principal would coach a teacher.
 • In what ways does a coaching school promote a calm and nurturing environment?

• • •

It's not just teachers and students who are involved in coaching. Principals and assistant principals must also participate—both with students and with each other. Setting up weekly or monthly coaching meetings to discuss what teachers are teaching, what students are learning, and what procedures are being implemented can help cultivate a cadre of learners at every level of the school community.

Students are not the only ones in school to learn. Teachers and principals may learn from each other as well as from their students. Sharing is the key to creating a school community that values and supports communication at all levels. Principals establish the standards for an egalitarian atmosphere, allowing it to flourish and grow. However, they must walk the walk as well as talk the talk: Teachers evaluate principals' levels of commitment to policies not by what the principals say, but by the actions that they take. Highly committed principals honor the methodology of coaching.

It is essential that principals model ways to obtain and share information in a variety of settings for teachers if teachers are to do the same inside their classrooms. When everyone talks about what they've learned, the directions they're taking, and what they can teach one another, the attendant synergy and vitality can motivate people to expand their intellectual horizons.

Case Study of Principal—Assistant Principal Coaching Using the GOPER Model

Meling, the principal, is speaking to Alison, the assistant principal, about preparations for an upcoming exam.

Meling: Alison, I am concerned about the ESL [English as a Second Language] department. The ELA [English Language Arts] test is coming up and I am concerned about whether we are preparing the students properly. The fact that many of our students are recent immigrants from Asia makes it difficult for us. What can you tell me about the teachers and students?

Alison: Well, I think there is a problem with knowing what each level means in the department. I think that we should give the teachers a list of what is expected of them at each level, from ESL 1 to ESL 6.

Meling: We want our teachers to take ownership of their departments. What could we do differently in order to get them to establish the levels, instead of imposing the levels on them?

Alison: I guess I could invite them to join me for a lunch meeting and ask them how they think the ESL levels differ.

Meling: An excellent idea [*compliment*]! What would you like them to discuss [*purpose*]?

Alison: I may want to consider asking each level's teachers to speak before the group and define what their level is and is not.

Meling: That would certainly open up better communication in the department. How will you know what they've done to prepare for the exam [*focusing on the goal*]?

Alison: That's a little harder because it will make them accountable, won't it?

Meling: Yes it will. Think about what you could request to better prepare them before speaking to the group [*understanding the options*].

Alison: I could ask them to take a few minutes and write what they are doing on paper before coming to the meeting [*creating a plan*].

Meling: By giving the teachers time, you allow them to reflect on their teaching. By having them write ahead of the meeting, you make them accountable for what they write [*eliminating roadblocks*]. We have a small budget left for food, if you're interested.

Alison: Great! I'll make the announcement at tomorrow's morning meeting. We will plan to have the ESL department meet for pizza and soda in the library on Friday.

Meling: Are you free at 1:00 p.m. on Friday to debrief [*reflecting*]?

Alison: Hold on, let me check. [Alison checks her organizer.] Yes, I'm free. I'll see you then.

● ● ●

When administrators and teachers get together to talk about their methods and strategies, they help cultivate a schoolwide coaching environment. Using coaching strategies with colleagues helps to further embed the concepts, helping teachers to be coaches rather than simply to think like them. When all levels of communication are open, whether vertically or horizontally, support becomes available from a variety of sources.

Case Study of Principal-Teacher Coaching Using the 3 Ps + C Model

Mario, a principal, notices that Rosa, a 5th grade teacher, is not acting her usual self. He invites her into his office to learn about what could be troubling her.

Mario: Rosa, you know that I think the world of you [*compliment*], but I have become concerned this week. I notice that you are not as focused in your teaching as you used to be. There is a big change in your performance from just last week [*purpose*]. I'm curious: what's changed?

Rosa: Mario, I have always thought of myself as a professional, and I don't want my personal life interfering with my teaching.

Mario: I want you to understand that I don't mean to pry, but I'm here for you. Whatever it is that's bothering you, you may want to consider sharing it with me so that you are not alone in whatever is happening to you. We've been at this school together for what, eight years now?

Rosa: My dog, Bernardo, died and I am just so distraught. He lived a good life, almost 20 years. I'm single, so Bernardo was always my companion.

Mario: That must be a terrible loss for you; it's understandable for you to be feeling this way. It's not easy going through the pain of losing a beloved pet. How can I support you?

Rosa: By doing what you're doing right now: letting me realize that my teaching is being affected. I just have to get a handle on myself. Some of my friends told me to go out and buy a new puppy, but I'm not ready yet.

Mario: I have a strategy that just might work for you. Would it be okay to share it [*permission*]?

Rosa: Please, anything that could help me. I know that what I'm feeling is normal, but I thought I would be a lot farther along by this point.

Mario: Rosa, what if you took those feelings of loss and used them to celebrate Bernardo's life? Here—please take a piece of paper and write down 5 to 10 things that you loved about Bernardo that made your life sweeter, livelier, or more fun. Take your time, there is no rush [*positive suggestion*].

Rosa: Okay. [She writes the list.] Here they are.

Mario: Tell me one of your favorite experiences with Bernardo—something that may have happened over and over again.

Rosa: Well, Bernardo loved to play fetch—the only problem was his own excitement. When he'd return the stick to me, he wouldn't let go. All he wanted me to do was to throw it again. He made me laugh so, as I'd pet his head.

Mario: Rosa, how have you shared your loss with your students?

Rosa: I haven't; I didn't feel that it would be professional.

Mario: Rosa, you have a warm and nurturing environment in your classroom. You love to write and you encourage your students to write all the time [*compliment*]. I can't think of a population that loves dogs as much as children and single adults do. Your students may help you move through this tough time. In what ways do you believe that your students may have dealt with losses in their own lives?

Rosa: I never thought of it that way. I'm sure they've had their own losses—grandparents, pets, friends, maybe something tangible that they cherished. You know, this could be a springboard for a lesson.

Mario: That's a great way to reframe what has happened to you. I can see the wheels in your head spinning, Rosa! Share with me what you're thinking.

Rosa: I may want to share the list I just wrote with my students. Hmmm . . . maybe I'll bring in a few pictures of Bernardo and me.

Mario: So, Rosa—you already look like you're on your way. When you walked in here, your shoulders were slouched and you seemed aloof. Now you're like a different person. Your spirit has kicked back into action and you seem focused again [*compliment*].

Rosa: Mario, I have to run. I hope you don't mind, but I have a lesson to put together.

Meeting personally with teachers, even if it's only five minutes every morning with the staff, promotes a bond that allows for feedback. For this reason among others, it is important for principals to walk the hallways each and every day and remain informed about what's going on at the school. Principals who are informed and who embrace progress will always be open to suggestions, and will find their efforts applauded. The more principals model a sense of progress, the more open the teachers become to taking risks, knowing that the effort alone is commendable.

Classroom Observations and Discussion Clubs

One way for administrators to encourage the useful sharing of strategies is to allow time for teacher-coaches to observe one another in action. Classroom observations can help teachers draw connections across the disciplines and spark ideas for approaching similar content in their own classes. Overlapping teaching strategies from classroom to classroom allows for a sense of continuity that students will come to expect and enjoy. It's not easy for students to go from an active classroom to one in which the teacher only lectures while the students take notes. If teachers are having a hard time implementing the workshop model or conducting project-based lessons, perhaps they need look no further than the classroom next door.

Teacher-coaches should have time in their schedules to get together and discuss teaching strategies. Administrators may offer teachers the opportunity to organize clubs around reading, gardening, sports, or any other activities that don't have "work" stamped all over them. A book club could focus on new young adult literature, so that teachers can share useful titles and discuss ways to get students reading and discussing them; a gardening club could focus on the science of plant cultivation, thus sparking ideas for a school garden or greenhouse; and a sports club could emphasize statistics, building bridges to the math classroom.

Summary

Every principal needs to help establish a course that has a clear purpose, and a mission of what the school should become. Students, teachers, and administrators jointly can establish goals for moving their school toward a coaching environment—when people have ownership in the process, they are more committed and motivated to perform. First, however, administrators must clearly articulate the school's values and model them by treating staff and students with the utmost respect, fairness, and compassion.

Section Summary

The focus of this book is to help increase students' and adults' abilities to "talk content" and write with a purpose. By acting as coaches, educators help students and colleagues to mature socially as well as academically, within a respectful atmosphere. Teachers should remember the GOPER plan when coaching students: Help them to focus on the goal, understand their options, create and implement a plan, eliminate roadblocks, and reflect on what they've accomplished. When teachers use guided listening and COACHing questions with students, the relationship between them will improve because the students will feel more successful as learners. In a true coaching environment, teachers and students produce a continuous flow of synergy: one creative idea sparks another, leading to motivation and engagement; students are complimented rather than reprimanded for solving problems in unusual ways. Most importantly, students begin to blossom, and the teacher-coaches get to see hidden talents come to fruition right in front of their eyes.

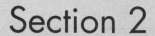

Section 2

Classroom Strategies

This section offers strategies for increasing discussion, deductive reasoning, and performance and art techniques in all subject areas. The section is broken down into the following four chapters:

• **Chapter 8: Discussion Strategies.** Strategies for helping students engage in conversation and "talk content."

• **Chapter 9: Deductive Reasoning Strategies.** Strategies for helping students investigate, pare content down to what's relevant, and use clues to unlock mysteries.

• **Chapter 10: Drama and Art Integration Strategies.** Strategies for helping students integrate performance and art techniques that let different types of intelligences shine through.

• **Chapter 11: The Nine Steps of Project-Based Learning.** The nine necessary steps for implementing the strategies in chapters 8–10.

Essential Question: What are classroom strategies that support a coaching environment?

Guiding Questions and Statements:

• Explain specific classroom strategies that encourage students to "talk content."

• Describe in detail how students will write for a purpose if they are personally motivated.

- In what ways can students work together so that they build on each other's personal strengths?
- Generate a list of strategies that promote discussion, debate, and simulation.
- Describe strategies that encourage the use of negotiation and problem solving.
- Describe in detail strategies that promote differentiated instruction and differentiated workstations.
- In what ways can we nurture the natural integration of the arts: drama, music, poetry, and fine arts?
- Specifically describe strategies that encourage students to perform in front of one another, thus fostering interaction and motivating students to learn.
- Explain in detail strategies that promote evaluation, synthesis, and analysis.

Discussion Strategies 8

Incorporating discussion strategies into the active classroom can help students enhance their speaking and listening skills. These strategies allow students to interact with their classmates, draw connections between what they read and what they discuss, and integrate new information, taking ownership of their own knowledge on a given subject. It s fun, too!

No longer do students have to sit quietly at their desks, awaiting their chance to speak. Discussion strategies require students to know the material, engage it in conversation at different levels, and work with others to build their knowledge. Teacher-coaches who incorporate varied discussion strategies will find their classrooms come alive with excitement: When every week offers a new challenge and a new strategy, students are motivated and eager to learn. Suddenly, the classroom hums with the exciting bustle of learning and sharing, as students bring their own special experiences to an intelligent discourse about what they have read and researched.

Accountable Talk

The Accountable Talk strategy (McKeachie, Pintrich, Lin, & Smith, 1986) cultivates students' abilities to speak in a compelling and persuasive way, preparing them to debate, lobby, and negotiate shrewdly. Accountable Talk is a secondary strategy—in other words, its function is to reinforce students' communication skills, while requiring that they assess their abilities to achieve their goals. (The primary teaching strategy would focus on the presentation and acquisition of content material.)

Accountable Talk can be incorporated into classroom activities that require students to speak and listen. Students are paired up and instructed to listen closely to each other as they make oral presentations. Listeners must assess their partners' performances on specific criteria, thus holding them accountable for what they say.

Once students know what they are to research and present, and the assessment criteria are negotiably contracted with the teacher, clear guidelines can be established as to what is expected from each speaker. Examples of acceptable criteria include actively speaking and participating, making eye contact, using prepared notes, asking important questions, using primary source documents, and responding to other speakers. Behaviors to be safeguarded against could include interrupting, engaging in side conversations, insulting others, veering off on tangents, or not responding to others' points. Students are supposed to explicitly list these as behaviors to avoid during the negotiation of criteria. The comparison helps to further clarify what is expected. Once the criteria are outlined, all students should receive observation sheets on which to assess their partners (see Figure 8.1). Before proceeding with the oral presentations, time limits should be set so that students can have time at the end to share their assessments. Of course, the teacher should model constructive criticism first, so that students don't insult one another. Once Accountable Talk has been incorporated into the classroom setting, teachers may modify the criteria over time to focus on skills that need particular attention.

Classroom Application

Here are some examples of how this strategy can be adapted to a variety of subject areas:

• Language arts students can conduct a forum comparing and contrasting the personalities and aspirations of heroes in the books they're reading.

• Science students can lobby for or against stem cell research, focusing on the moral, scientific, and economic issues involved.

• Social studies students can debate the merits of building and maintaining a nationwide railroad system.

Figure 8.1

Accountable Talk Observation Sheet

Directions: Each time your partner does one of the following, place a check in the box.

Your partner's name: _____

POSITIVE

Actively speaks and participates:

☐☐☐☐☐☐☐☐☐☐☐☐☐☐☐☐☐☐

Responds to another speaker:

☐☐☐☐☐☐☐☐☐☐☐☐☐☐☐☐☐☐

Asks quality questions:

☐☐☐☐☐☐☐☐☐☐☐☐☐☐☐☐☐☐

Refers to his or her notes or any text with pertinent information:

☐☐☐☐☐☐☐☐☐☐☐☐☐☐☐☐☐☐

Makes eye contact with the person who is speaking or listening:

☐☐☐☐☐☐☐☐☐☐☐☐☐☐☐☐☐☐

NEGATIVE

Speaks in a bullying fashion:

☐☐☐☐☐☐☐☐☐☐☐☐☐☐☐☐☐☐

Interrupts another speaker:

☐☐☐☐☐☐☐☐☐☐☐☐☐☐☐☐☐☐

Engages in conversation on the side:

☐☐☐☐☐☐☐☐☐☐☐☐☐☐☐☐☐☐

Does not stay on the topic:

☐☐☐☐☐☐☐☐☐☐☐☐☐☐☐☐☐☐

Puts others down:

☐☐☐☐☐☐☐☐☐☐☐☐☐☐☐☐☐☐

Describe in detail the points that your partner made that were most interesting to you:

Describe in detail what you would have said in the discussion if you were given the chance:

This flexible strategy can be built into any classroom and prepares students for a world that requires them to speak in open forums, listen to others, respond to varying perspectives, and respect their peers.

Flexible Jigsaw

As its name implies, this strategy is particularly flexible, as it embraces both homogeneous and heterogeneous groupings. The strategy basically requires teachers to "jigsaw" students from homogeneous groups to heterogeneous ones.

Getting the ball rolling is easy. First, the teacher divides the class into groups of five. Each group gets a reading assignment that is appropriate to the students' reading level. The groups may be asked to meet once or twice a week until the reading is finished. For homework, each group should read a portion of its designated reading assignment. Though each group has a different selection to read, the students should all answer the same open-ended question. Examples of questions that students might answer include the following:

Fiction
- "Describe in detail the conflict that confronted the main character."
- "If you were a friend of the main character, how would you help him?"
- "Describe the setting and how it affects the characters."
- "Describe the tensions between the main character and the other characters in the book."
- "List the qualities that you share with the main character, and the ones that you don't."

Nonfiction
- "Describe in detail the main purpose of the reading."
- "In what ways does the reading represent a specific viewpoint?"
- "For what reasons can or can't you trust the reading?"
- "In what ways is the document one-sided?"
- "How does this reading help you understand a particular time and place in history?"

Teacher-coaches can also generate questions with input from the students, after they've learned active listening skills. They can then provide students with monthly reading schedules ahead of time, helping the groups make their selections of particular book choices.

Once the students have all answered their first question about the reading, the groups should convene to discuss their responses, learning from one another while clarifying aspects of the text that they may have found confusing on their own. After they have had a chance to discuss their readings, the students should count off from *A* through *E*, then jigsaw from their original homogeneous groups into new, heterogeneous groups—*A*s grouping with *A*s, *B*s grouping with *B*s, *C*s grouping with *C*s, and so on. In these new groups, each of which contains a representative for each of the readings, the students share what they've learned from the reading and work on answering the same open-ended question.

Because each student is the sole representative of her reading selection within the new group, her contribution to the group carries the weight of authority; the playing field is thus made level, with struggling readers as respected as gifted ones. At the end of the class period, students should report to their original groups and briefly present the highlights of their discussions to the entire class.

Once or twice a week, the teacher-coach should post a new question and assign new readings. Students may be asked to keep a reading journal where they can record their answers to the questions, respond to the readings in their own words, and highlight any interesting points they may want to take up with their groups. They could also reflect on what they learned in their heterogeneous groups, using the opportunity to write about what they learned about the other students' readings. They may also be asked to reflect on how their material relates to the topic of the lesson, drawing links that they can then discuss with their groups.

When the readings have been completed, the teacher may ask students to write a paper on how the readings are relevant to real life. (For example, they may develop profiles of two characters, one fictional and the other real, and compare and contrast them.) This activity can be applied in countless ways.

Teacher-coaches may be pleasantly surprised to find that this flexible group arrangement can actually be an incentive for students to read the other selections discussed in their heterogeneous groups. The Flexible Jigsaw strategy is noteworthy because it allows for both homogeneous *and* heterogeneous groups to take part in the same task.

Classroom Application

Clearly, the Flexible Jigsaw strategy can be incorporated into most subject areas. In language arts class, selections could be primary sources from a historical period, young adult literature selected with a specific theme, or support readings for major works. For instance, if the class is reading *Lord of the Flies* and studying the themes of power and evil, the teacher-coach may incorporate one of the following pieces of fiction for each group: *Downriver* by Will Hobbs, *Killing Mr. Griffin* by Lois Duncan, *The Drowning of Stephan Jones* by Bette Greene, and *The Chocolate War* by Robert Cormier. (Social studies teachers could use these titles too, in conjunction with unit themes such as leaders and followers, good versus evil, backstabbing, or anti-Semitism.)

Teacher-coaches of social studies might arrange groups in a Civil War unit around such titles as *The Red Badge of Courage* by Stephen Crane, Harriet Beecher Stowe's *Uncle Tom's Cabin,* or *The Narrative of the Life of Frederick Douglass.* Alternatively, they could use primary sources, such as the Gettysburg Address, authentic journals of Union and Confederate soldiers, newspaper clippings from the era, and so forth.

In science class, if the topic is nuclear energy and weaponry, students may be asked to read such selections as *Phoenix Rising* by Karen Hesse, *After the Bomb* by Gloria Miklowitz, Robert C. O'Brien's *Z for Zachariah*, or Caroline Stevermer's *River Rats*. All of the books deal with nuclear power or the aftermath of a nuclear war. Primary sources might include John Hershey's *Hiroshima*, nonproliferation agreements among nations, and statements made by leaders and scientists from all over the world.

Students will welcome the Flexible Jigsaw strategy as a break from textbook readings and will appreciate the opportunity to escape into the world of historical fiction or authentic primary sources. With flexible reading groups, the whole class can be pulled into the pages of exciting literature, regardless of ability level.

Lobbyist Hearing

The Lobbyist Hearing strategy (Stix, 1998a) is not just for the social studies classroom. This simulation requires students to act as lobbyists representing four different points of view. They don't have to defend positions with which they agree, but they must make their presentations believable, persuasive, accurate, and meaningful; after all, their goal is to persuade a panel to agree with their point of view. Role playing is fun for students, and the forum of the simulation can vary—possible venues include a town meeting, a union hall, a political party conference, a book club, a science conference, a legislative assembly, or a PTA meeting. A panel of judges represents the listeners and decision makers for each hearing. "This is a very good strategy to use for teaching how to cooperate in negotiating contracts or highlighting a particular position," said teacher Abbu Hinckson-Martin of Queens Academy High School.

There are some prerequisites to the Lobbyist Hearing. First, the subject under discussion must have at least four different perspectives available for defending—two "pro" and two "con." Second, background sheets need to be prepared for each point of view. These highlight key information regarding each point of view and provide students with a starting point for their own research. Third, students should be organized into as many groups as there are points of view. Once these three criteria are set, the activity may begin.

The teacher-coach should ask the students to describe a time when someone tried to persuade them to do something or think a certain way. They should discuss the issue among themselves, and then determine what their experiences had in common. They should describe in detail how they were convinced and what techniques the speaker applied. The teacher should then call upon one group at a time so that each may offer one response, rotating from group to group.

Next, the coach should describe the simulation to the class. Students now have to persuade each other to take their point of view on a controversial topic. In addition to reading their background sheets, students should be required to conduct additional research at the multimodal and multilevel classroom workstation independently and to identify key points together. The strategy works best if teacher-coaches are already familiar with classroom workstations that hold a variety of texts, manipulatives, and other materials for student use. "Going to various stations to find supporting information allows students to be exposed to different perspectives," said Queens Academy High School teacher Darryle Cook. Students can also use the library, Internet, or other resources to prepare the best case they can for their assigned positions. They will craft a speech meant to persuade and convince their listeners, and take turns speaking.

Once the students have a good idea of what the strategy involves, they may negotiate the criteria for assessment. Sample criteria may include addressing key issues, having an initial stronghold, capturing the audience's attention, sequencing the argument effectively, closing with a provocative ending, speaking persuasively, and sticking to the point. Some students might privately indicate to the teacher that they are uncomfortable with the role they have to play or with the point of view they have to espouse. In this case, the teacher-coach might compare the simulation to a play, in which all the students take on roles for what is being staged. The students must be advised that they will be evaluated on how well they play their roles—in other words, on how effectively they get their point across to the audience. Their personal opinions and convictions are never at issue. Who today would argue the merits of slavery as tenaciously as did the slaveholders of the Confederacy? Yet this is exactly what is expected of the students: that they speak as eloquently for those with whom they disagree in reality as they would for those with whom they agree. The point of the Lobbyist Hearing strategy is for students to better appreciate the fact that there are two sides to every story, and to learn to tolerate what others have to say. The strategy gives students a better understanding of the world that existed in the past as well as the one they live in now.

Students should read their assigned perspective and become familiar with all of the major debating points. The more research they seek out, the more they will know; teacher-coaches should make it clear that if the students do not venture beyond the information sheet, they are bound to miss out on much relevant information that could help sway the panel. The teacher-coach may assign open-ended homework questions or statements to help students decide how to present their positions and organize their thoughts. Examples include the following:

- "For what reasons do you consider your point of view important?"
- "Compare and contrast the weaknesses and strengths of your point of view."
- "Describe in detail all the major points you are trying to express."
- "Generate a list of important facts."
- "List in detail all the strategies you will use to get all your points across to the audience."

When their research is done, groups should discuss what they have found with each other. Students should prepare charts, graphs, photographs, primary sources, and other visuals to support what they will say in the forum.

Members of each group should then be assigned a letter. Once everyone in a group has a specified letter, the students should be jigsawed into new groups, with all *A*s sitting together, all *B*s sitting together, and so on. Each person shares a perspective with the other members and listens carefully. This part of the activity is important, since it allows students to gain an understanding of the opposition they will face before fashioning a line of argument. It also allows the students to get an overview of all the complex issues involved, and a more rounded appreciation and understanding of the opposing sides. (Some teacher-coaches may decide to give all groups all the information sheets so they can be aware of the counterarguments ahead of time, but this is best suited to advanced classes.)

Now that students have become privy to multiple views, they should move back to their original groups and discuss what they have learned about the other perspectives. This strategy ensures that students are constantly "talking content" and building their knowledge through the sharing of information. These groups become experts on their perspectives by discussing both their own point of view and the opposing ones. They can anticipate other arguments, strengthen their own, and be prepared with counterarguments.

Following this group discussion, the teacher-coach should ask the students to brainstorm all the ideas they can generate regarding their perspective and write them on an organizational sheet. Next, they should decide which points to cover in their presentations. They may decide to cover all of the points, or just those that they consider most salient. When they have done this, they must decide on how to sequence their arguments, starting with a strong opening. At this point, students must agree on which points each of them will cover and write brief speeches, between 30 seconds and one minute in length, covering their points. (Alternatively, the teacher may decide to require a full-length speech from every student, as a way of incorporating more writing.) Each student should cover a different point and should be instructed to include a "hook"—something that grabs the listener.

Once they write their speeches, the students should make note cards with just the key words written on them. Having entire sentences written out might tempt the students to read from the cards, and this should be avoided at all costs. There is nothing more disheartening than watching a student with head bowed low, reading his speech. It is the student's job to win the listeners, not just through persuasive speech but also by maintaining eye contact and using gestures that convey emotion. Before beginning the simulation, students should be asked to generate a list of what constitutes good speaking behavior (e.g., eye contact, differing levels and tones of voice for emphasis, gestures showing emotion, appropriate body language).

One day before the lobbyist hearing, one student from each group should be pulled out to serve on the panel. To avoid a tie at the decision stage, there should always be an odd number of panel members. Students chosen for the panel should leave their notes with their groups, who must then incorporate them into their speeches. As the groups do this, the panel members should discuss their different perspectives and agree to put them aside and to listen with open minds. They should also use this time to create a list of open-ended questions they will want the speakers to answer after each of their presentations.

The teacher-coach may ask the students to dress the part on the day of the lobbyist hearing. They could dress as professional lobbyists, or they could be asked to dress in the appropriate manner of the group they are representing. For instance, if they are portraying Roman senators and Carthaginian envoys seeking to convert the Italians to their side during Hannibal's invasion of Italy, they could all wear togas. The students can also bring whatever props they might need, along with charts, graphs, and pictures, to create a realistic setting for a serious and dignified hearing.

The lobbyists are now ready to begin. The panel sits in the front of the room behind desks with paper and pens, ready to take notes and pose questions. The groups assemble, and the teacher-coach announces that the hearing will come to order. The panel members introduce themselves. The first lobby group meets at the side of the room, so that both the panel and the other groups can see them when they make their presentations. This allows the speakers to stand in such a way that they can maintain eye contact with everyone in the room. A speaker who keeps his back to many of his listeners has already lost a large segment of his audience.

As soon as a representative from the first group announces their position, the students in that group begin their speeches, using any visual materials they have to substantiate what they say. The other groups take notes on the presentations and chart the information. After each of the first group's presentations, one panel member asks an open-ended question, which one member of the lobbying group answers. Once the first group finishes, the teacher-coach helps the students reflect on how well the group performed. The coaching element helps increase the proficiency level of the groups that follow. In this strategy, the coach acts as the moderator, sets the pace of the proceedings, keeps time, and assesses the class by filling in a rating chart specific to the activity that is based on the criteria negotiated earlier.

After the first group has presented and the teacher-coach has helped the students reflect, the process is repeated with every group. The moment of truth comes when all the groups have finished their speeches. The students on the panel are excused and leave the room to discuss what they have heard; based on their cogitations, they render a decision. Meanwhile, the groups convene to predict what the panel will decide. When the panel reenters the room, one member announces the verdict.

The hearing is not yet over, though. Once the verdict is announced, the students shift gears and pretend to be members of the general public who have just been informed of the outcome. They should discuss alternative solutions that may incorporate some views from the different groups, or that they may have formulated from their own follow-up brainstorming. After listing the alternative solutions, the class generates a comprehensive list and votes on which ones seem the best, as the teacher-coach charts the results.

Of course, no lesson is complete without reflection and a writing exercise. For homework, teacher-coaches should ask students to reflect on the hearing and pose open-ended questions to themselves; they should then answer these questions in writing, thoughtfully considering other possible responses. The students should be graded on the quality of their questions and answers.

In class the next day, students should share their responses with their cooperative groups and discuss their experiences in the lobbyist hearing. As a postactivity, students can be asked to find out what controversies are brewing at the local, state, or federal level. Many cable stations air debates and speeches on various issues, and students can learn from the various techniques employed. In class, they may then discuss what they have observed.

Classroom Application

Applying the Lobbyist Hearing strategy to different content areas is easy. In language arts class, the students can try to sway a panel of judges as to Gene's guilt or innocence in Finny's fall from the tree in John Knowles' *A Separate Peace*. One group could defend Gene, arguing that he did not shake the tree on purpose and that it was simply an inadvertent happenstance. Another group could argue that Gene was guilty, trouncing the tree on purpose and acting out a fit of jealousy toward Finny. A third group could present the opinion that while Gene probably did trounce the limb on purpose, he did so subconsciously, with his conscious self unaware of his urge to do so. Finally, a fourth group could argue that there was no way to tell one way or the other, and that a decision regarding Gene's guilt or innocence could not legitimately be reached without further evidence. Sigmund Freud would beam with pleasure listening to students discuss all these psychological issues.

"[The Lobbyist Hearing] is my favorite strategy because I can see the students being excited and willing to participate . . . [in lessons on] Supreme Court cases and U.S. foreign policies," said teacher Paula Rosa-Gerstein of Queens Academy High School. Possibilities for using the Lobbyist Hearing strategy in social studies class are endless: independence versus loyalty to the crown during the Revolutionary War, Andrew Jackson versus John Calhoun, the merits of the Wilmot Proviso, labor unions versus Big Business, isolationism versus involvement in World War II, and the pros and cons of the Iraq War are all potential debating topics.

In science class, students might debate such pressing topics as global warming, dependence on foreign oil, the harvesting and sale of human organs, and funding for NASA and other government agencies.

The Lobbyist Hearing strategy has kids "talking content" in various ways at every step in the lesson. They learn from each other and themselves as they brainstorm, analyze, synthesize, and relay information to different groups of listeners. They cooperate to meet their goals, and they write responses based on their newfound understanding.

Stix Discussion

The Stix Discussion (Stix, 1998b) incorporates an inner-outer circle forum, with students in the outer circle feeding notes and clues to their speaker-representatives in the inner circle, who argue the issue. This multilevel discussion strategy is participatory and exciting, and, more importantly, it gives every student an active role to play.

Teacher-coaches begin by organizing students into groups. Informational sheets representing four perspectives are distributed to the groups, so that each student in a group has a different perspective. Students review their points of view, then jigsaw into new groups where everyone has the same perspective. Of course, they are now expected to become experts on their points of view through further research and group discussion. Once they do this, they return to their home-base groups and share what they have learned.

When the teacher-coach tells the students that they will be participating in a Stix Discussion, the negotiable contracting of criteria can take place. Examples of appropriate criteria include addressing key issues, making good eye contact, speaking convincingly, using primary and secondary sources to support points, using visuals to illustrate a point, listening well, and actively participating without overwhelming the rest of the group. The teacher may assign open-ended homework questions or statements to help students decide how to present their positions and organize their thoughts. Examples include the following:

- "For what reasons do you consider your point of view important?"
- "Compare and contrast the weaknesses and strengths of your point of view."
- "Describe in detail all the major points you are trying to express."
- "Generate a list of important facts."
- "List in detail all the strategies you will use to get all your points across to the audience."

As always, students should be aware of how they are being assessed. They should be given enough time to research their perspectives and to discuss strategies for the Stix Discussion. All the while, the teacher-coach circulates the class acting as a coach, notepad in hand, offering guidance and charting the actions of the students.

On the day of the discussion, the teacher-coach arranges one small circle of chairs in the center of the room. Behind each chair are two or three additional chairs, also facing the center of the circle, creating a larger outer ring (see Figure 8.2). The number of chairs depends on the size of the class; in a class of 24 students, the inner ring would have 8 chairs (2 for each perspective) and the outer ring would have 16 (4 students acting as aides for each inner-circle pair).

Figure 8.2

Setup for the Stix Discussion

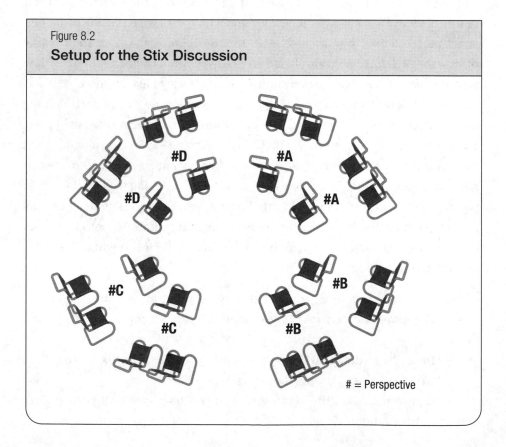

There should be small pieces of paper, perhaps 2- by 3-inches in size, on top of each chair in the outer ring. Only the students in the inner ring are allowed to speak; those in the outer circle may pass notes to the speakers, but may not speak themselves. Some teachers may ask students to initial the notes they pass, for assessment purposes during the simulation. Each member of the group should be assigned a number before the simulation begins. Later, when the inner and outer circles rotate, all 1s and 2s who initially sat in the center ring will move to the outer circle, while 3s and 4s move in, with the rotation repeated as often as necessary until all class members have the opportunity to take part in the discussion.

Before the discussion begins, teacher-coaches should remind students of the assessment criteria to which they agreed. The groups may also wish to take five to seven minutes to discuss the points they want to make beforehand. As a warm-up, the coach may want to conduct a two-minute practice run, so that everyone understands the process.

The inner circle begins the discussion. Students take turns speaking about their point of view, making sound arguments for their side, addressing and countering the points made by the opposition. This goes on for three to six minutes, with the outer ring of students passing notes to their partners in the inner ring.

As the outer circle consists of the aides or clerks, they are not allowed to speak. They must carefully listen and write down suggestions that they want to offer to their inner-circle partner. Once written, they should tap their partner on the shoulder lightly. This individual, who may not turn around (to not lose eye contact with the rest of the peers in the inner circle), raises and opens his hand. The student in the outer ring should place the note cautiously into the palm of the hand. This way, the speaker is not taken away from the discussion. The teacher-coach tells the students in the outer ring that they are not allowed to pass a note while their partner is actively speaking. They should wait until their partner is finished speaking before tapping the shoulder.

When the time has expired and the first inner circle has finished, the teacher-coach helps the class reflect on how well the group performed; this helps increase the level of proficiency for the next round of discussion. The coach uses authentic assessment as noted in Figure 8.3 for grading purposes. The negotiable contracting criteria can be used to make the students accountable for what they say and how they discuss the topic. The teacher can use a point system (1–10) or a check system ($\sqrt{}$++, $\sqrt{}$+, $\sqrt{}$, or $\sqrt{}$-) for each criterion. Students can assess each other if peer assignments are made.

Figure 8.3

Authentic Assessment for the Stix Discussion

Topic: Date:	Addresses Key Issues	Clarity of Speaker	Listening Skills	Eye Contact	Supporting Evidence
1. Lashawn					
2. Pablo					
3. Tina					
4. Timmy					
5. Maylee					

Next, the coach signals that the second round of speakers should take their place in the center ring. Once all students have had their turn to sit in the inner circle, the teacher-coach may decide to call anyone who has been hesitant or quiet to join the center ring again, this time without being overwhelmed by more active or dominant speakers.

When all views have been exhausted, students should jigsaw back into their home-base groups, where all viewpoints are represented, and collectively decide on some possible outcomes by discussing, listing, and ranking their ideas. The class as a whole can then discuss the ideas and chart them on the board. The groups must decide on a single solution, possibly incorporating related ideas. Here is where "writing for purpose" comes into play: The teacher-coach asks the students to write formal recommendations for solving the dispute, either individually or as a group. They should also follow up with a written reflection on what they learned from the exercise about considering different viewpoints and making decisions.

Before concluding the lesson, the class should discuss the real-life outcome of the examined controversy. Students can determine if their solutions were better, worse, or the same as what actually happened.

Classroom Application

Many subjects lend themselves well to this strategy. The strategy is even applicable to language arts classes, where literature is the main focus. Students can discuss whether or not the protagonist of *Maggie: A Girl of the Street* is responsible for her own downfall or was deliberately abandoned by those who should have sheltered her.

In social studies class, students can debate the pros and cons of James Marbury's petitioning the U.S. Supreme Court for a writ of mandamus to secure his government appointment, or the measures the Florentine city council should implement to alleviate the scourge of the Black Death in the Middle Ages.

In science class, they can debate whether the sale and consumption of alcohol should be restricted or banned, or determine whether it is morally acceptable to experiment on animals.

Creative Controversy

There are many politicians who are notorious for changing their opinions on issues. This tendency, which journalists commonly refer to as "flip-flopping," is a notable presence in many heated political campaigns. In the Creative Controversy strategy (Johnson & Johnson, 1995), students begin by taking one side of an issue, and then switch midway to the opposite viewpoint.

The students first draw initial conclusions based on their limited experiences, personal perspectives, or ways of organizing information. When they share their personal rationalizations with others, they engage in a cognitive rehearsal that allows for a deeper understanding of their positions; thus, when they have to take the opposing position, it causes conflict and turmoil. The material that they had previously absorbed must now be manipulated differently—by recasting, reorganizing, reclassifying, and reordering—to support the new point of view. Though this process creates an initial feeling of uncertainty, by the end of the experience the students will have sharpened their reasoning skills and attained a higher plane for making sound, knowledgeable judgments. Both Ruggiero (1988) and Johnson, Johnson, and Smith (1997) concluded that forums where students use higher-level reasoning and critical thinking lead to superior teaching, so this strategy is a challenge that benefits both teacher-coaches and students.

The coach should prepare for the exercise by bringing up a subject for debate and providing the students ahead of time with informational sheets reflecting two competing points of view. These sheets should highlight key points about each perspective, providing students with a starting point for their own research. Next, the teacher-coach should explain to the students that they will begin with one view and then switch to an opposing view.

When students understand what they must do, the negotiable contracting of criteria can take place. Examples of acceptable criteria include addressing key issues that go beyond the information sheet, holding the listener's attention, sequencing the arguments effectively, responding with clear and precise citations, using good listening and responding skills, listening respectfully to an opposing opinion, speaking persuasively and making a lasting impression, and staying with the point of view.

The teacher-coach should divide the students into groups of four. Two students are assigned the *A* position, and the other two are given the *B* position. Using multimodal and multilevel workstations, the local library, the Internet, and other available resources, the students research and prepare the best case they can for their assigned position. The students are motivated because they know that they are writing and preparing for a simulation that will actually take place in the classroom. Upon completing their research, students write down key points on index cards to help them during their debates, using only one or two key words and avoiding phrases and sentences. Because each group has two students who share the same position, they can assist each other. During the debate, both students must make equivalent presentations; they may speak for equal lengths of time, or divide their speeches into categories, taking turns addressing each one.

On the day before the debate, it is a good idea for the teacher-coach to model the Creative Controversy strategy with two students in front of the class for about two minutes. The topic should be mundane (e.g., "Is grounding an effective punishment for teenagers?"). At the end of the modeling session, the teacher-coach can ask the class to critique what it did and did not find effective. This pre-activity dialogue will help them understand what it means to use good listening skills. Among other observations, the students might point out what is essential or significant in the speech, what left a lasting impression, how the use of proper supportive materials strengthened the speech, and why it is beneficial not to belittle the opposition. Once the process has been modeled, students can make their last-minute preparations.

On the first day of the Creative Controversy debate, the *A* pair from each group makes its presentation, and the other pair engages in active listening, taking careful notes. After the initial presentation, the *Bs* ask the *As* questions during a Q&A. Applying the benefits of their active listening the *Bs* may restate what they heard or question certain parts of the presentation for greater clarity. The *As* and *Bs* then switch places, and the process begins anew.

For homework, students must now get ready for the next day's activity by reading the information sheet and preparing adequately for the opposing position. On the second day, all *As* take on the perspective of the *Bs*, and vice-versa. The students make their presentations, followed by the Q&A. The second day often proves to be meatier than the first, because students have had the first day to lay the groundwork and the homework assignment to probe for more details. This is where students are expected to add new facts and to elaborate upon the initial presentations.

At the conclusion of both presentations and Q&A sessions, the four-student home-base groups should convene and participate in an open discussion. By engaging in an open forum, the students can synthesize the evidence from both sides and use their reasoning skills to tap information at a higher level. The group can openly discuss the strengths and weaknesses of both positions, and even try to create a single position by integrating elements from both sides. Students think beyond the constraints of the positions they were locked into at the start and have the chance to create a middle ground that may be more realistic. They may see a new way of looking at the evidence or reorganize pre-existing conceptions.

Whatever they do, the students are now looking at both positions with a more open-minded view, even if their personal positions have not moved in any dramatic fashion.

Throughout the Creative Controversy strategy, the teacher-coach's role is to circulate from group to group and assess how well the students are doing. She can intervene and use coaching skills when needed, to bolster confidence, help brush aside obstacles, and generate enthusiasm.

The Creative Controversy strategy challenges students to use higher-level reasoning and critical thinking. Having students take positions on both sides of an issue and then reach a harmonious consensus helps students to shun physical confrontation in a world already filled with conflict.

Classroom Application

Topics that easily lend themselves to the Creative Controversy strategy abound in all of the disciplines. In language arts class, possible subjects could include which authors should receive the Nobel prize, which characters from different novels are the greater villains, or (more specifically) whether Don Quixote is a demented fool or a blessed saint.

In social studies, academic issues such as the right to die, regime change in the Middle East, free trade in the Western hemisphere, and human rights vis-a-vis U.S. foreign policy are all suitable topics.

In science class, students can take positions on such contentious issues as force-feeding of anorexics, DNA databases for criminals, the legalization of drugs, the dangers of corporate pollution, and disposal of hazardous waste.

Magnetic Debate

The Magnetic Debate (Stix & Hrbek, 2002a) puts students in the position of enthusiastically and expertly "Talking content" with each other. Though the topics may be serious, it is a fun activity nonetheless. The teacher-coach first decides on an issue that has two distinct viewpoints and that is complex enough to be broken into categories. Each student is given a specific category to research according to one of the points of view. The students should know ahead of time that they will have to synthesize their written arguments into a larger whole, so that they can envision the final results of their research. When students understand that their work will be displayed in front of the class, the quality of their compositions is elevated. Though the teacher can always assign the positions himself, allowing students to choose on their own gives them a degree of ownership and motivates them to excel.

The class is divided into four groups: one for each of the two opposing viewpoints, one consisting of a panel that will pose questions, and one of students who do not know which side to take. The two opposing groups meet at opposite sides of the room, the question-panel group sits at the front of the room, and the undecideds sit in the middle (see Figure 8.4). Though undecided, these students must still conduct general research in order to become familiar with the issues. The teacher passes out informational sheets for both perspectives, giving everyone a general starting point.

Figure 8.4
Physical Layout for the Magnetic Debate

Pro   Undecided   Con

Interrogation Committee

The primary objective for each side is to convince the undecideds of its position. When the first side is called, a speaker makes a one-minute presentation about whichever category she has been assigned. Her counterpart on the opposite team then does likewise, following which the first speaker is allowed a one-minute rebuttal. The question panel then asks both speakers clarifying questions. When the speakers are finished, the undecideds may move their chairs closer to the side they are beginning to favor. Once the category is completed, the teacher-coach helps the class reflect on how well each student performed. As with the other strategies in this chapter, integrating the coaching element helps increase the level of proficiency for the upcoming presentations.

The two sides take turns initiating the debate with each category; after each category is presented, the undecideds move their chairs closer to the side that they favor. Oftentimes, students move their chairs in one direction at the beginning, only to move in the opposite direction as the debate moves into full swing. When all the speeches have concluded, the side with the most chairs closest to it wins.

Teacher-coaches should save some time at the end of class or on the next day for a postdiscussion about the Magnetic Debate. Students can describe the new things they learned, indicate which side or what particular student made the most compelling arguments, and discuss why they finally chose to stand with one side in opposition to the other. While these classroom discussions are taking place, the coach may chart the findings on the board using a Venn diagram, comparing the major points that were made by each side. Students can then be assigned a follow-up paper that compares and contrasts the opposing positions, with the objective of understanding both. This can be either an individual or a group activity; teacher-coaches must be open to what works best for their students.

When teacher-coaches incorporate a wide range of resources and strategies, they often find that underachieving students reverse their poor performance. This is because students are writing for a purpose—to prepare for the simulation that is to take place—and, later, to reflect on what happened during the simulation.

Robert Wagner Middle School 7th grader Lauren Schneider thought the Magnetic Debate strategy was valuable. "It enabled me to feel as though I was a part of history, present at actual historical events, making the same decisions and taking into account the same considerations that led these real people to take the steps they did," she said.

Classroom Application

In language arts class, students reading the books *Catherine, Called Birdie* and *Lyddie* might use Magnetic Debate to learn more about women's rights through the ages; categories might include male domination, domineering father figures, family pressures, marriage choices, educational opportunities, work satisfaction, and equal pay.

In history class, teachers might use the Magnetic Debate strategy for a mock debate between Athenians and Spartans during the Peloponnesian War, with each side seeking to convert the city-state of Argos into an ally. Categories for discussion could include education, treatment of women and foreigners, attitudes toward citizenship, and military training.

In science class, students might debate the merits of hybrid automobiles versus SUVs. Categories could include efficiency, passenger safety, design, environmental friendliness, emission standards, and economic impact.

Four Corner Debate

In this activity, students are required to take a stand on an issue that allows for gradations of support. The strategy shows how students' views begin to change as they listen to one another, changing their minds when challenged by new ideas.

To set the stage, the teacher-coach asks students whether or not they have ever changed their minds while growing up. A student might state that he hated eating peas when he was five, but finds that he now enjoys munching on raw peas during the summer. Another student might admit to being terrified while watching scary movies when a child, but now enjoys going to the movies with her friends when a new thriller has just been released. The teacher himself might add that he used to only buy modern furniture, but with time has grown to appreciate antiques. The objective here is to highlight the fact that changing one's mind is healthy, that our minds are not dormant, and that we are not static thinkers.

Next, the teacher-coach explains the Four Corner Debate strategy: The coach will pose a question, and each corner of the room is labeled with different responses. At first, students will go to a corner where their opinion is shared by others. They will share their experiences with their peers. After reading a relevant passage or hearing a shared reading by the teacher, the students will then jigsaw into new groups to discuss the passage. Afterward, they may return to the same corner or switch to a different one, depending on whether they have been persuaded by the reading or their peers to change their minds.

Once the objective has been explained to the class, the teacher-coach embarks on negotiating criteria of assessment with the students. Such criteria may include speaking briefly and clearly, using persuasive techniques, being respectful and attentive, listening when someone else is talking, and taking appropriate notes.

As preparation, the teacher-coach places a different poster at each corner of the classroom, reflecting four possible reactions to a position: strongly disagree, disagree, agree, or strongly agree. Then the teacher may assign a reading to the students for homework and have them say which of the four reactions they had to the position stated in the reading. Students should write down why and how they came to their decisions. The next day, the teacher-coach should ask them to go to the corner that reflects their decisions. If the coach has selected an issue that can claim sophisticated gradations of support, there will be students in each corner. The students are then urged to discuss in depth why they made their selections and to take notes when their classmates speak. The teacher-coach should circulate from group to group, making sure that students are using the skills discussed during negotiable contracting and facilitating when necessary.

At the end of the discussion, students should count off from 1 to 4, 5, or 6, depending on the number of students at each corner. (If a corner has eight students, they should count off 1 to 4 twice.) The teacher should then jigsaw the students into new groups according to number, where they are to cite examples from the text and try to be as persuasive as possible within a specified period of time (four to eight minutes, let's say). The teacher continues to coach the students, circulating from group to group and making sure they are on task, trying to give the necessary help, and also assessing how well they are meeting the negotiated criteria. Students should speak with enthusiasm, but also be brief in their statements; no one student should hog all the time. When two students represent a particular view, each should be given the opportunity to speak. During the numbered group discussion, it is important for students to continue to take notes.

After the first jigsaw, the teacher-coach asks the students to reflect upon their notes and to make a new decision as to how they feel about the issue at hand. They may return to their original corner, or they may change their position and walk to a new corner. When all students have made their decisions, they should share with one another why their positions remained the same or why they changed their minds.

This activity can be repeated with a new reading, or by having the students discuss something they saw on TV.

As part of the reflection, students should take part in a whole-class debriefing: For what reasons did their positions remain constant? In what ways did they change? Were they more likely to listen to someone who made excellent points, or to someone who was just babbling a lot of hot air?

Students should use their notes from the activity to write a concise paragraph stating their opinions on the issue. The students should note whether they strongly disagree, disagree, agree, or strongly agree with the position they have read, then list at least four points to substantiate their decisions.

Classroom Application

As with the other strategies in this chapter, the Four Corner Debate is applicable to all subject areas.

In language arts class, students might debate whether Helen of Troy was truly worth "the launching of a thousand ships" in *The Iliad*.

In social studies class, students can debate whether or not Abraham Lincoln was the greatest president to hold office.

In science, students might debate the merits of dissecting animals in high school versus simulating the procedure online.

In music class, students can debate whether or not Elvis Presley was responsible for merging the blues with gospel and country music; different pieces of music can be played after each sequence of the strategy.

In physical education, students might debate whether Gene Kelly or Donald O'Connor in *Singin' in the Rain* or Fred Astaire and Cyd Charisse in *The Bandwagon* were the most accomplished dancers. After each jigsawed experience, the teacher may choose to show a different clip of the movies, or different dancers, such as Gregory Hines, for the students to analyze.

Regardless of the topic, the Four Corner Debate strategy is an exciting activity. The teacher-coach can see the intellectual growth of the students as they move from place to place, actively participate in discussions, and take a firm stand on an issue that was intellectually dissected and satisfactorily engaged.

Negotiations and Settlements

Knowing how to negotiate and settle problems is an important skill all students should learn and practice from an early age. Making compromises and concessions, standing firm on important points, and evaluating offers and decisions are all imperative to the negotiation process and important facets of "talking content." In literature, characters often make compromises, whether with themselves, with others, or with the world, that illustrate or change who they are. In science, researchers must often negotiate with governments, corporations, and others to make breakthroughs in important areas. And, of course, among the nations of the world, treaties, compacts, agreements, and alliances are often struck like bargains, where each side has a say and where no side usually gets everything it wants.

Learning that compromise and negotiation is an important part of life is one of the key outcomes of the Negotiations and Settlements strategy (Stix & Hrbek, 2001a). It encourages students to use their powers of persuasion, evaluate information, build strategies and alliances, and make decisions based on the best interests of those they represent. This strategy can stand alone or be used as a concluding strategy to the Lobbyist Hearing, Magnetic Debate, or Stix Discussion strategies. In any situation where differing perspectives vie for prominence, the Negotiations and Settlements approach will generate enthusiasm and make the classroom a lively place.

As in other strategies, teacher-coaches should provide students with informational sheets about the issue to be discussed, which should be based on a historical case. Of course, students are required to go beyond these basic informational sheets and conduct their own research. In addition, the teacher-coach should prepare an overhead transparency titled "Outcome of the Negotiation," "Settlement Agreement," or something similar.

Working in groups of four, students are given the informational sheets to review. Half the students in each group work on one perspective, and the other half work on the other. They review the information, conduct additional research at home or at the multimodal and multilevel classroom workstation, and carefully prepare points to discuss. They are told they are to act as negotiators, delegates, ambassadors, lawyers, or whatever roles make the most sense for the material at hand. Their job is to reach an agreement that is acceptable to all sides and to report the final results to the class. When each group has presented its settlement, the whole class will vote on which group reached the best solution.

Now that students understand the task, the negotiable contracting of criteria can begin. Some sample criteria for assessment include working collaboratively, using persuasive and respectful language, achieving a reasonable compromise, and using outside resources to bolster their positions. Because they will be expected to write a proper agreement, criteria for that aspect of the task should also be discussed and agreed upon. Some criteria that could be used to assess the written agreement include clear and succinct writing, accurate representation of the negotiation, proper sequencing and organization, and use of compromise and negotiating skills.

The negotiations are ready to begin at this point. The teacher may devote one class period to understanding the dilemma and having students prepare their positions. The next day, students should be given approximately 30 minutes to negotiate and 15 minutes to write their treaties (times can be modified to suit the class length). The conflict resolution strategy that we offer here is modified from Jewish Women International. It is broken down into four steps using the acronym SOCS, which stands for situation, options, consequences, and solution:

S = Situation. The situation is well defined; students know who, what, where, when, how, and why the problem exists.

O = Options. Each pair brainstorms a list of options from its perspective. No judgments should be made at this stage; it is more important to be free-flowing and to generate as many options as possible.

C = Consequences. Each pair reviews its list, prioritizing the items and starring those that are most essential. Are the items all-or-nothing options, or are there gray areas? Students should discuss all of the consequences, both positive and negative, for each item on the list.

S = Solution. Both pairs now come together and negotiate the items on their lists. Their objective is to negotiate a settlement, meaning that both parties leave the table feeling that they have accomplished something and designed a mutually satisfying solution. Failure means that one or both parties were not flexible enough, few compromises were accomplished, and no real gains were made. If the students prepare properly and work hard at compromising, their efforts will be noteworthy.

While the students are involved in their negotiations, the teacher-coach circulates the class as a coach, notepad in hand, giving guidance and charting the actions of the students. When the time is up, the class joins together once again. Each group is called upon to present the outcome of its negotiations. When every group has offered its thoughts, the class should vote on which agreement was the best. Students can even rank them all in order and discuss what made one group's negotiation stronger than another's.

Finally, the real-life outcome of the dispute should be presented to the students. They may be surprised at the results, and may even believe they have devised a more suitable solution themselves. For reflection, the teacher-coach may ask them to write a journal entry comparing and contrasting the actual settlement with their own proposals, or to reflect upon a time in their lives when they had to negotiate for something of value. For homework, students can be asked to find treaties or agreements currently being negotiated in troubled areas of the world. The important thing is for students to take a hard look at how negotiations aid the process of globalization and contribute positively to the world community.

Tess Nanavati thought the interactive nature of the Negotiations and Settlements strategy was especially appealing. "I learned to think and act like a person from that time period who is trying to make an important decision," said the Robert Wagner Middle School 7th grader. "It wasn't just copying something off the board—*I was actually part of it.*"

Classroom Application

Students may not be aware that reporters often must negotiate with subjects of news stories for access to information. As part of the writing curriculum in language arts classes, the Negotiations and Settlements strategy can be used to acquaint students with the role of the investigative journalist. For instance, in the O. J. Simpson trial, there was some discussion of whether or not cameras and reporters would be allowed into the courtroom. In this case there were more than two sides involved: there were the defense, the prosecution, the journalists, the court officials, and the families of the victims. Classroom discussions could address such issues as public access, impartiality, and the effect of celebrity on the legal process. As a writing exercise, once the negotiations are complete, students may be asked to put themselves in the roles of reporters on the case. Writing for a specific purpose will motivate students to conduct further research.

The Negotiations and Settlements strategy is clearly useful in the social studies classroom. It can be applied to any locale plagued by war, as well as to any scenario in which different sides come together to negotiate contentious issues. For instance, when studying the Cold War, a teacher may present the two major sides in the conflict and how they reached agreements limiting the arms race. One side could represent the United States and its NATO allies, while the other could represent the Soviet Union. The student negotiations should take place before the real-life outcomes are taught in class.

In science class, the strategy could be used when studying the mapping of the human genome. Students may take on the roles of those representing the private and public sectors involved to determine how best to share (or even whether to share) information with each other and with the public.

9 Deductive Reasoning Strategies

Learning to use deductive reasoning strategies to solve problems is not easy. Although students may use reasoning and logic every day, they are not likely to be aware of it. When teachers emphasize the use of deductive reasoning strategies and encourage critical thinking and analysis, they allow students to explore their own approaches to problem solving and decision making. Asking students to reflect on how they come to their conclusions is paramount, as it helps students to become aware of their own thinking. Such metacognitive approaches to learning help students to discover new ways of looking at situations.

The strategies in this section encourage teachers to emphasize deductive reasoning in a variety of settings and subject areas. These strategies are like scavenger hunts: Using information from a specific historical period, students use the clues to determine and understand contemporary counterparts.

Hidden Clues

Many students like to watch TV shows that feature detective work and forensics. Teacher-coaches can use the deductive reasoning skills displayed in such programs and put them to work in a classroom setting. The Hidden Clues strategy, also known as

Concept Attainment (Taba, 1971), gets students to make connections among content, both independently and as a whole class. Students must use logic to determine why information is categorized in a particular way. In this student-centered strategy, concepts are formed, clarified, and used as a foundation for further knowledge.

As preparation for the Hidden Clues strategy, the teacher-coach should consider a topic and generate a list of ideas that students are likely to know about it. The potential ideas should then be categorized under general topic headings. (For example, when studying the human body, a teacher may come up with various subheadings and specifics for the different systems.)

Next, students should be divided into groups. The teacher-coach presents the topic and asks the class what they know about it. The students then reflect privately and write down their thoughts. After two minutes, the members of each group should be asked to share their ideas with one another and consolidate their information. The coach then asks each group to offer one idea at a time, going from group to group. The ideas are charted on the board or on chart paper, with the teacher strategically grouping related ideas together in columns without making any note of particular headings. The process of eliciting responses continues until most ideas have either been charted or examined and eliminated. At this stage of the strategy, it is extremely important to make sure that students do not talk in their groups, as one student could ruin it for the entire group. Students will be motivated to figure out the strategic groupings of ideas. When all ideas have been exhausted, the teacher asks students to supply headings for the groupings she has written. At this point, students may come up with some very broad headings, but they may also begin to see some subheadings coming out of the broader topics.

Once this task is completed, teacher-coaches ask students what they observed in this activity. Perhaps they will notice that they had to first analyze and then synthesize information to find common bonds. Perhaps they will see the hierarchies that exist in the relationships. Perhaps they will draw a variety of conclusions and generalizations about the topic and the strategy in general, and about how they think and organize information. Whatever they come up with, they are talking and they are thinking.

Classroom Example

We found an excellent example of this strategy at work in an elementary school. Teacher Maria Bonitello asked students to write down 10 words that start with the letter "c." Rotating from group to group, she asked each student to share a "c" word with her. She began to chart all of the words, but in different columns. At first the class looked puzzled and asked her what she was doing. Ms. Bonitello answered that if they paid very close attention, they would be able to figure it out.

At first, Ms. Bonitello's list looked like this:

| clap | chariot | cellar | candy |
| crackle | chicken | citizen | coins |

The students in her class remained puzzled. However, with many more additions, the list expanded and began to look like this:

clap	chariot	cellar	candy
crackle	chicken	citizen	coins
cracker	cello	cider	cat
cross	ciao	cent	carve
cry	chocolate	ceramics	carnival
clay	chubby	city	cable
cramp	church		cave
	chopsticks		cavity
			cash
			cartwheel

Before long, students were raising their hands and saying they knew what Ms. Bonitello was doing. She continued a little further until the enthusiasm to explain the groupings really swept through the classroom. She decided to call upon individual students, one at a time, to select and explain one column each. The first student said that the second column from the left had a "c" that when coupled with an "h" sounded like "ch." Smiling, Ms. Bonitello labeled the column. The second student said that the third column had a "c" that sounded like "s." The third student said that the fourth column had a "c" that sounded like "k." At this point, one student asked why the fourth column was separate from the first column, which had words like "clap" and "cross," where the "c" had a similar "k" sound. Another student, enthusiastically raising his hand, replied that in one column, the first two letters were consonants and blended together, whereas in the other column, the "c" preceded a vowel. Another student inquired about the second column: Why did the "c" words "cello" and "ciao" have a "c" followed by "e" or "i," but sound like "ch"? Ms. Bonitello laughed. She said that when she created this exercise, she only thought about English words, but these words were of Italian origin. She explained that different languages have different rules. By the end of the class, the students discovered by themselves the pronunciation rules for the letter "c."

Classroom Application

This strategy can be applied to various subject areas. In language arts, students may be asked to list all the features they can think of about poetry. The information can then be organized into groupings based on types of poems (e.g., lyrical poems, sonnets, limericks, free verse) and reorganized into "schools" of poetry (e.g., classical, modern, beat). In an end-of-the-year review, students can list all of the great fictional protagonists that they read about in short stories, novels, or plays.

In social studies class, students may be asked what they know about the 1960s. Information may first be organized into groupings based on themes (e.g., Civil Rights, the Vietnam War, the Great Society, presidential decisions, the counterculture).

In science, teacher-coaches can use the strategy to explore the periodic table, listing all of the elements and then having students categorize the classifications as they are being written on the board.

Deliberations

In the Deliberations strategy, also known as the Case Study Method (Silverman, Welty, & Lyon, 1992), students read a story that offers many insights into a specific situation. The students' task is to deduce information, relying primarily on their analytical skills, and to comprehensively delineate each person's perspective as set by the parameters of the story. Once the roles have been defined, students can discuss an open-ended question posed by the teacher.

The most difficult part of this strategy is probably selecting the story. The basic requirement is that the story has great detail, offering many different connections among people and circumstances. The writing should offer an intelligent and complex plot, with insight into the various characters and how they respond to events. Of course, the story must lead the students to the open-ended question that is posed for discussion.

The teacher-coach divides the class into cooperative groups, then distributes the story to each student, either for homework or to be read in the groups. At this point, it is extremely important for students to realize that their initial judgments and speculations will probably change throughout the procedure. The teacher should let them know that once the analysis of the story has been completed and all discussion exhausted, they then can begin to form their own opinions. It is essential that students keep an open mind. The coach explains that they will first analyze each viewpoint and then scrupulously examine each of the characters in the story. Only then will they discuss the open-ended question.

Once students are aware of the elements of the assignment, the criteria for assessment can be discussed. Criteria could include obtaining appropriate information for each viewpoint or character, listening and responding well to others, clarifying one's position by referring to the text, and taking proper notes of the discussion.

General Viewpoints

The first task is to take a point of view and to generate a list of pros and cons for it. Let's say the story is about a teenager who seeks to be admitted to the after-school science club, which designs special projects that are submitted to prestigious national competitions. The teenager does not meet the highly selective requirements to be admitted to the club, but makes a solid case for being allowed to participate, based primarily on his enthusiasm for science class.

Many different viewpoints can be generated from this example, including those of administrators, parents, teachers, and student groups. For each view, students should generate a list of pros and cons. The teacher-coach circulates from group to group, assessing how well students are discussing and analyzing the information and offering guidance when needed. Once the groups have analyzed each viewpoint, the teacher charts the responses on the board.

Character Analysis

The next task is for students to analyze each of the main characters in the story. In our example, the principal may only want students who have been on the dean's list to be accepted into the science club. Perhaps the science teacher is an outspoken advocate for the teenager because the two of them share a special connection. The teenager, who normally is not motivated by teachers, is excited about a subject for the first time; he wants to make the effort to succeed and enjoys the sense of control over the learning process that he feels in science class. The teenager's parents might be outraged that an after-school club would be so elitist, while other parents may feel that a homogeneous club helps challenge students more.

The teacher-coach continues to provide services to all of the groups as they discuss each of the characters. Once the groups have analyzed each character, the teacher uses active listening and charts the responses on the board.

Discussing the Issue

Students must now turn their attention to the open-ended question—in this case, "Should enrollment in the science club be open to all who apply?" Students list their opinions in groups, creating a T-chart of the pros and cons of admitting everyone to the science club. The teacher uses active listening and charts the information on the board. Once all groups have offered their responses, the groups discuss the information in detail and come to a conclusion.

Some students might note that, say, there are four pros but only two cons, resulting in an imbalance. The teacher-coach should note that perhaps some points carry more weight than others. Because there is an even number of students, each group can negotiate. This is an inducement for the students to compromise and use their negotiation skills to arrive at a satisfactory conclusion.

As an extension of the deliberations, students should write position papers reflecting on how their group cast its vote. They may end their writing exercises by stipulating the exact reasons they agreed or disagreed with their group. It is important for the teacher-coach to reflect with the students by asking them in what ways their opinions changed during the course of the assignment. For what reasons was it easy or hard for them to refrain from giving an opinion initially? They should generate a list of reasons for playing devil's advocate.

Classroom Application

Any number of stories can be used in the Deliberations strategy. In language arts, students can pause midway while reading *Twelve Angry Men* by Reginald Rose to deliberate what they think will be the final outcome.

In social studies class, they might read about Senator Joe McCarthy being honored with a Citizenship Award in the 1950s. The Deliberations strategy is a wonderful way to air issues that are often litigated in a courtroom.

In a science or geography class, students might read about a landfill being planned for a residential community.

Making Decisions

In the Making Decisions strategy (Stix, 2002), students make decisions by plotting a novel or recreating history, step by step. They must determine what steps should be taken at a particular time and place, deciding the fate of a literary protagonist or historical figure.

Ahead of time, the teacher-coach prepares "decision cards" that list the sequence of events in a given narrative. Each card should end with a point at which a decision must be made and should offer two to four possible decisions for the students to choose from. (If four choices are offered, students should rank them in order of preference.) The next card in the sequence reveals the actual decision that was made in the narrative and continues with the story.

Students are required to record their responses to each card and provide a rationale for their decisions. This way, they are asked to evaluate, synthesize, and justify their choices based on logical thinking. They discuss the content with one another and listen carefully to opinions from their peers.

The Making Decisions activity can be conducted in pairs, groups, or a whole-class format, with groups of four acting together to determine a choice they will offer the whole class. Before beginning the activity, the teacher-coach should provide students with some background information on the story to be examined. Students should be told they will be taking on leadership roles and must make decisions based on the information provided. Once the activity is explained clearly, the criteria for assessment are negotiated. Assessment criteria may include active participation, weighing and judging choices before rendering a decision, offering meaningful rationales, supporting other suggestions, and respecting the views of others.

If the teacher-coach decides students should work in pairs, one set of cards should be distributed to each pair. If the whole class will be working together, an overhead transparency can be made for each section of the story. In pairs, students read the cards, discuss the choices, and together decide on a course of action, recording their choice and rationale. The teacher-coach circulates through the room, helping students to discuss their choices and decide upon options. In the whole-class format, one group is called on to read the information, and then all groups discuss the choices and make a decision; two or three groups can then be called upon to explain their decisions and they should be prepared to support their choices with sound reasoning. When decisions have been made, the next card can be examined. At this point, the answer to the previous question is revealed, and students can see whether or not they made the "right" decision in comparison to the one reflected in the story.

At this time, the teacher-coach reflects on the process, asking if any group or pair wants to share any good decision-making methods with the class. Then the activity resumes: the students continue until all of the cards have been read, with the teacher rotating the groups called upon to elicit their responses. All the while, the coach assesses their performance based on the criteria determined earlier.

As a modification to the basic activity, students may be asked to rank their choices. The teacher-coach asks which groups chose choice A, and those groups provide their rationales to the class. Then the groups that selected choice *B* are called and asked to present their reasoning. This process continues for choices *C* and *D* and is repeated with each subsequent card. At all times, the coach circulates from group to group, coaching the students, offering guidance, and assessing their performance.

Students should be made aware that men and women in leadership positions are often called upon to make crucial decisions; in the case of government officials, they will often be required to decide issues of life and death. Young people know they will have to make crucial decisions for themselves at some point. As a reflection exercise, students can write journal entries describing decisions they have had to make in their lives, and how they arrived at those decisions. Their writing should include the options they considered, why they chose to go one way as opposed to another, what the outcomes were, and how the decisions affected their lives. Alternatively, they may be asked to write an essay comparing and contrasting their own decisions to those made in the story they examined.

Classroom Application

In language arts class, students may be given the plot of a story ahead of time and asked to predict its course before reading the book or a particular section. This is a useful strategy for difficult readings; the intellectually challenging format of the activity makes great literary works more understandable. For instance, a Shakespeare drama can be cut into short sections and written in prose for the students to consider. When students compare and contrast their responses with what happens in the play, they are able to synthesize and evaluate materials on a higher level.

The Making Decisions strategy is of exceptional value when discussing wars between nations in social studies class. When studying World War II, for example, students may be asked to put themselves in the place of Franklin D. Roosevelt to decide whether the United States should remain neutral after Hitler's invasion of Poland.

In science, students can place themselves in the roles of doctors and scientists working on cures to for of the world's illnesses. They must make life-and-death decisions about funding for research, which illnesses to address first, which drugs to develop, and so forth.

Vote On It!

Because students will be voting throughout their lives—whether at work, in the family circle, or at local, state, and national elections—voicing well-formulated opinions based on facts emerges as a lifetime skill. Responsible voters do not cast their ballots haphazardly, but rather arrive at choices by weighing all the options and examining the evidence.

In the Vote On It! strategy (Stix, 1993), students are presented with a selection of four to six "candidates," all of whom are suitably qualified for a given job. As part of the preparation, the teacher-coach provides each group with candidate cards, written out in the form of a brief resume describing each person in detail. The true identities of the candidates should remain a mystery until the activity is finished. The teacher-coach should keep an answer key on hand that lists the actual achievements and attributes of each candidate, and display it at the end to reveal the candidates' true identities.

The activity is now ready to begin. In groups, students read the candidate cards and discuss each applicant's qualities and characteristics. The students must decide on both the best person for the role and the worst, and provide reasons for their choices. Talking about the content enlivens the classroom; some students may find themselves debating the qualifications of their favorite candidates. The teacher-coach circulates the room, giving guidance to each group.

When each group has made its choices, the teacher charts the responses on a bar graph, using one chart for the most favored choice and one for the least favored. When the charts are done, each candidate is discussed individually. Those who voted for the candidate in question as the best should offer their reasons why, as should those who voted the candidate as the worst.

When every candidate has been discussed and all students have spoken, the teacher-coach reviews the overhead transparencies for the individual candidates, revealing just one point at a time about each person—their achievements, failures, personality characteristics, and so on—before finally uncovering the individual's true identity.

As a reflection exercise, students should be asked to consider how their choices differed from the reality. They may be asked to write a resume for the candidate of their choice, making the case for why that individual should have been chosen instead. If their decisions match reality, they can elaborate upon the qualities that made their choice the best, or write a letter of recommendation for the candidate. This way, students can see the purpose for putting forth the best case for a person's qualifications. This is a process they will have to do again themselves, at least mentally, when casting ballots in the future.

According to 7th grade student Andrew Schulz of Robert Wagner Middle School, the Vote On It! strategy was eye-opening. "It made me more aware of where I come from and how [the United States] became what it is today," he said. "It made me aware of who I am and what rights I have as a citizen."

Classroom Application

In language arts class, students might try to find out which of several characters in Hemingway's *For Whom the Bell Tolls* are true heroes.

In social studies, they might evaluate the generals being considered to head the Pentagon's Joint Chiefs of Staff.

In science class, they might consider NASA's candidates for the first manned U.S. spaceflight.

Identity Crisis

Although the teenage years are fraught with anxiety, this lesson is not about asking students to find out who they really are. The Identity Crisis strategy (Stix, 1993) allows students to find out more about historical figures, literary characters, or concepts through a series of questions and answers. Students must use deductive reasoning to determine the identity on "identity cards."

To begin the lesson, the teacher-coach provides students with an informational sheet about people, characters, or concepts. Students are asked to review the information for homework and to become thoroughly acquainted with each item on the list. They may be asked to extrapolate the most notable characteristics of each item, as a way of moving information from short- to long-term memory. In the meantime, the teacher prepares mystery cards that contain information on an even number of profiles. Each card should include the name of the person or concept being identified, along with a list of attributes, achievements, and responsibilities. A picture of the person or item can also be included. Sets of the cards should be made for each group (for management purposes, each set should be photocopied onto different colored paper).

During the next class session, the teacher divides the class by the number of cards; for example, a class of 24 students divided by 8 profiles would yield 3 groups of 8 students. Students are told they will each be given a different identity card, to be taped on their backs, and that they will work in their groups with those who share the same colored paper to determine their identities.

Once the cards are distributed, students walk up to someone in their group and ask three yes-or-no questions about their identity. When the questions have been answered, they rotate to a new person in their group. The answers should be based on the information they have on their cards. For example, if the activity centers on Greek gods, questions might include: "Am I a woman or a man?" "Do I rule the underworld?" "Am I a great hunter?" or "Am I known for my great beauty?" Moving from person to person encourages all members of the groups to talk to one another. This is very important, because "talking content" is the only way for the students to achieve their goals.

Once every group member has talked to every other group member, students may guess their identities, or, if they cannot, they may repeat the process, this time asking open-ended questions to gather additional information.

Of course, once the teacher-coach has described and modeled the activity, the class should negotiate the criteria for assessment. Important criteria could include asking logical questions, working with all members of the group, listening and responding to questions carefully, and providing helpful answers. When the activity begins, the teacher circulates the classroom and assesses students in their roles as inquisitors and responders. After the first five minutes, the teacher-coach freezes the activity and asks the students to assess their progress. After students ask any clarifying questions and the teacher shares any observations, the activity resumes.

Upon completion, when everyone has guessed their identities, the whole class may reflect on the exercise and what they learned about asking questions and deducing answers based on gathered information. In their journals, students should reflect on the experience by posing an open-ended question about the activity and answering it in a meaningful way. They will be assessed on the quality of the question as well as the answer. Writing about their experiences reinforces the process of deduction through intelligent questioning.

Classroom Application

This activity can be used for any language arts, science, or social studies unit in which various persons or characters are studied. In language arts class, it works particularly well for learning Greek, Roman, Nordic, or Asian mythology. It also works as a follow-up activity to units on works with several major characters, such as the writings of Charles Dickens.

Because most historical periods are dominated by several prominent figures, the activity works especially well in social studies class. Students can review such figures as Lincoln, Jefferson, Washington, or Roosevelt.

In the science classroom, the identities to be guessed could be elements from the periodic table, with the properties and most common compounds for each element described on the cards. This activity can also be applied in biology, to examine mammals, reptiles, birds, fish, and insects.

In short, the Identity Crisis strategy can be used for any subject in which multiple items with various attributes are studied. It's a novel approach to learning that intellectually engages students while also making the classroom a fun place to be.

The Real Deal Game

Throughout the ages, stereotypes have been used to identify and discriminate against those whom we do not fully understand and, therefore, fear. Even today, as much as we take pride in the advances we've made by educating people, stereotypes persist. By encouraging an awareness of various stereotypes and showing that they are seldom applicable in any rational way, teacher-coaches can sensitize students to the harmful effects of such generalizations and reinforce efforts to teach understanding and tolerance.

The Real Deal Game strategy (Stix & Hrbek, 2002c) encourages deductive reasoning based on the gathering of information and intelligent questioning. It requires careful attention, a high degree of familiarity with materials, and the ability to make rapid comparisons and contrasts.

The teacher decides ahead of time on two stereotypes to be examined. For instance, she may choose to look at the Gibson Girl of the Gilded Age and the flappers of the Roaring Twenties, two stereotypes that existed one after the other at the turn of the early 20th century. It is important to choose stereotypes that are at opposite ends of the spectrum, thus making the case for gradations in between. As part of the preparation, the teacher makes a comparison chart, delineating the similarities and differences of both stereotypes, as well as a background sheet about them. Next, she creates profile cards for four fictional characters: one representing the flapper, one representing the Gibson Girl, and two others that combine gradations in between. Each profile is given a name; the information on the cards adds an element of reality and humanity to the fictional personalities. The teacher should make one copy of each profile card (preferably laminated for repeated use).

Before the simulation begins, the teacher-coach should ask students to think about stereotypes by posing several open-ended questions, such as the following:

- "For what reasons do we label people?"
- "Describe in detail what it is like to be labeled."
- "In what ways have you or someone you know been labeled?"
- "Describe in detail your feelings when you were labeled and stereotyped."

Working in groups, the students brainstorm their answers. The teacher-coach calls on one group at a time to respond and makes a master list of all the answers. Having introduced the idea of stereotypes, the teacher may now discuss the two under scrutiny. The background sheets on the stereotypes are distributed, and the teacher asks students to read them and to fill in a comparison chart with the characteristics of each. (Make note that the teacher first created the chart in order to write the stereotype background sheets; now, the students are reading the background sheets to fill in the chart.)

Next, the teacher indicates that everyone will review both the background sheets and the comparison charts for homework the night before the simulation. The class objective will be to decide, from the four profiles that will be presented the next day, which one is the "Real Deal" stereotype. In our example, they would have to decide which two of the four profiles are the "real deal"—that is, which ones correspond to the stereotypes of the flapper and the Gibson Girl.

Privately, the teacher selects four students to represent each profile in front of the class. These students are given the profile cards and are asked to memorize information about their characters for homework. The teacher should tell them that they are not allowed to talk to anyone about having been selected for the activity, or it will spoil the simulation. For this reason, it is best if these students are approached before or after class.

The negotiable contracting of criteria can now begin, as students understand their goals. Acceptable criteria could include asking quality questions, organizing information based on answers, listening attentively, the use of vocabulary associated with the particular stereotype, and speaking clearly.

On the day of the simulation, the four preselected "actors" sit at the front of the room, dressed as their characters if possible. The rest of the class ask questions and take notes on the answers. If the teacher has props, they can add flavor to the activity. Each group is allowed to ask one question to only two of the actors. This process rotates from group to group. After the first two groups have done their part, the teacher-coach asks the class what strategies they should use to help them analyze the information. Some might state that each group should follow the previous group's line of reasoning. Another suggestion might be to use active listening and chart the characteristics of each actor.

When every group has chosen which two profiles correspond to the stereotypes under consideration, the teacher asks the first actor to stand up and then asks the class whether they think she is the Gibson Girl, the flapper, or neither. Students vote, and the teacher tallies the results. Then the second contestant stands, and another vote is taken. Spokespersons for each group should rotate when each of the votes is taken. When all of the votes have been cast and tallied, the teacher-coach asks each of the actors to stand and reveal his or her true identity to the class.

In their cooperative groups, students should reflect on the simulation and what they learned about stereotypes. By discussing the content and learning from one another, they are better able to synthesize the lessons and teach one another about the dangers of assuming that people fit squarely into categories. (After all, just because the authors of this book wore bellbottoms and tie-dyed shirts in the 1960s doesn't mean they were hippies.)

For homework, students may be asked to write a journal entry, posing an open-ended question about the activity and answering it in a meaningful way. Or they may craft an essay comparing and contrasting the two stereotypes and analyzing why neither can be 100 percent accurate. When writing with a specified purpose in mind, it is important to have a meaningful outcome. To this end, students could design a magazine with feature articles about historical figures who either exemplify or are the total opposite of the stereotypes discussed. The assignment could also include writing about other stereotypes that have persisted up to the present day.

Classroom Application

Although this strategy works best for social studies classes as outlined above, it can also be adapted for language arts: The goal can be modified to identify characters from a novel, or to relate certain characters from a novel to a given stereotype in history, thereby linking language arts to social studies. Drawing connections between two different subject areas reinforces both and helps students to recognize the links between art and life, fiction and reality, and all of society's obstacles. For instance, when reading Edith Wharton's *The Age of Innocence*, students may be asked to review profiles of the Countess Ellen Olenska and May Archer in conjunction with the stereotypes of the flapper and the Gibson Girl. During the Real Deal Game, students are asked to identify Ellen and May and to decide if either or both correspond to the stated stereotype. The other two characters can be from the novel or made-up figures; if they are from the novel, students may be asked to identify all four characters and decide whether any of them fit the stereotypes. Writing assignments may include a comparison/contrast essay, a journal entry written in the voice of one of the characters, or a letter from one character to another regarding stereotypes.

In social studies class, such topics as who is a hippy or who is straight during the 1960s could be explored. Or students could decide which people in the Middle East were truly Hellenistic, in the centuries following the death of Alexander the Great.

Taking a Survey

Most students have seen, heard about, or even participated in some type of survey. They can be fun, and they provide us with an opportunity to be heard. Most are the very basic yes-or-no types of surveys, but there are other types that measure degrees of responses, allowing for shades of gray. Getting at these more varied thoughts is, in the final analysis, what's most important.

The Taking a Survey strategy (Stix, 1994) asks students to conduct a survey related to the topic they are studying and to chart their results. Most will find that even where there are degrees of difference, the charted results will resemble a bell curve, with most responses (but not all) tending to fall somewhere in the middle, rather than at the extreme ends. Designing the survey, asking people to participate, and analyzing the results entail patience and careful planning. The teacher can explain what the students should expect as they conduct their surveys, using an illustration of a bell curve as a model.

To begin, the teacher should model an example that is easily charted and understood—say, a model of different climates in the United States. First, students might be asked to individually write down their favorite climate and to specify a matching temperature range. On the board, the teacher-coach should draw two lines, one vertical and the other horizontal. The class is asked to imagine the entire population of the country answering the same question. Along the vertical line, the designation "Population" is written, with the line notched and numbered with increments of 50, each representing thousands of people. Along the horizontal line, labeled

"Temperatures," are set indices of 10-degree increments ranging from 0 to 100 degrees. Now, the class is asked to consider how many people live in the coldest climates, such as Alaska. With most students accurately guessing that the region has a small population, a mark can be made above the 30, close to the line. Taking a city such as Los Angeles, where there is a very high population density and the temperatures are relatively warm, a mark can be charted close to the top, around the 70-degree line. After going through a host of other cities and states with which students are familiar, the bell curve comes together in a visual diagram, the point of which will be clear to students: Most people live in the temperate climates, not the extremes. (See Figure 9.1 for an example of a climate chart.)

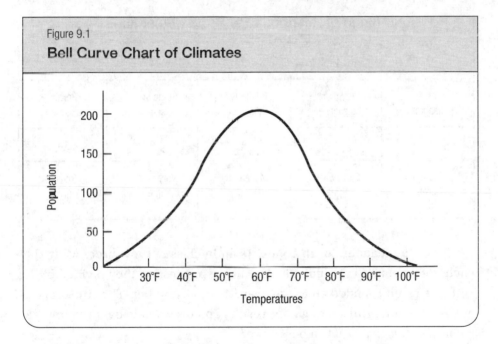

Figure 9.1
Bell Curve Chart of Climates

For the lesson itself, the teacher tells students they will be conducting a survey related to the topic they are studying in class. First, the students privately come up with a list of related questions that they might like others to answer. Next, they share their ideas and consolidate their lists in their cooperative groups. Using the active listening strategy, the teacher-coach circulates from group to group, asking for their suggestions and charting the results. She should then choose one of the students' suggested questions and, together with the whole class, design a model survey with sample responses. There should be gradations to the answers. For example, if the question is, "Do you agree that all types of guns should be available for purchase and use by any citizen above the age of 18?" responses should range from "Totally agree" to "Totally disagree," with other shades of opinion in between, such as "Barely agree," "Mildly agree," or "Moderately agree" (see Figure 9.2). Each possible response should be given a number from 1 to 10. Students should predict the responses before the teacher calls for them.

Figure 9.2

Possible Range of Responses to Survey Questions

1	2	3	4	5
Totally disagree	Very much disagree	Moderately disagree	Somewhat disagree	Barely disagree

6	7	8	9	10
Barely agree	Somewhat agree	Moderately agree	Very much agree	Totally agree

Next, the teacher-coach conducts an in-class survey, pretending that each vote counts for 10 individuals. The responses are then divided by 10, with the result rounded up to the nearest whole number. The students create a bar graph representing their results and draw a line over the top (see Figure 9.3). Does it create a bell curve?

The teacher should ask the students to speak with a minimum of 30 people when they conduct their surveys, to ensure a fair sampling. They will then consolidate their responses in groups. Students will be expected to chart their results, write their findings, draw conclusions based on what they found, and present their findings to the rest of the class.

Now that the students understand what is expected of them, they should negotiate the criteria for assessment. Criteria might include posing good questions, getting gradations of responses, having well-organized

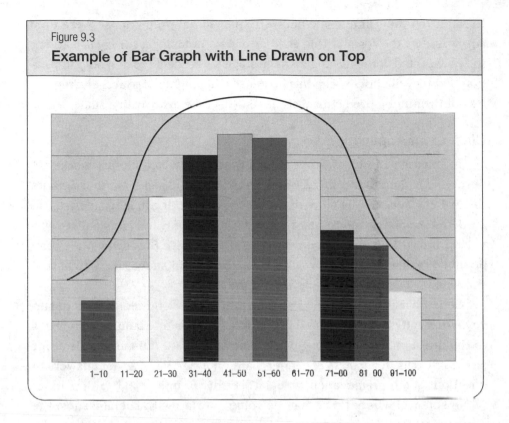

Figure 9.3

Example of Bar Graph with Line Drawn on Top

1–10   11–20   21–30   31–40   41–50   51–60   61–70   71–00   81 90   91–100

survey reports, providing strong introductions and conclusions to find-ings, graphing and labeling results clearly, discussing responses in detail, predicting the responses, and reflecting on the actual outcome.

The activity can now proceed. The teacher-coach rotates from group to group, listening to what the students have to say while asking questions and making sure that their questions and responses are appropriate for the assignment. Before conducting the survey, the students should make their predictions. This motivates them, making the survey more fun and excit-ing. If they will be surveying the community, the teacher must be certain that students never leave the building unless they are in a group and give the teacher their exact location. We recommend that the teacher exit the building with all the students, place them within a two-block radius, and constantly circulate the area to supervise them.

Once they have collected their samples, students create a graph and write their results. As with all the other activities in this book, students need to reflect on their findings. What were their initial predictions? Were they supported by the results? One exciting aspect of taking a survey is learning the unexpected. If the teacher sets the stage for students to find out information that they did not expect, this becomes a highlight of the activity; regardless of their initial predictions, students will come away with a smile.

Classroom Application

In language arts class, surveys might focus on which literary works are deserving of the Pulitzer Prize, or which of the world's great authors merits the Nobel. There can be more of a slant toward writing in language arts, so students may be asked to place themselves in the role of journalists surveying and writing about a current issue, reviewing a Broadway play, composing a review of a controversial book, or crafting a feature article that explains the purpose of the survey and the results.

Because many social issues and current events lend themselves to surveys, this activity is ideal for social studies class. For example, responses to the question, "Should the government reinstitute the military draft for all U.S. citizens, regardless of gender?" are bound to vary, as are answers to questions about privatization of Social Security or universal health care.

In science, where there may be some overlap with social issues, the surveys can ask for respondents' opinions on whether donated organs should be available only to those who can afford to pay, or whether animals should be subjected to medical experimentation.

Surveys require students to think critically about issues and to recognize that intelligent people do not simply say "yes" or "no" to issues of consequence. The wide spectrum of shadings that can be offered as answers to a challenging question illustrates for students the complex nature of humanity. Students will come away from this activity with a greater understanding of life's complexities, and an awareness that very few topics are as simple as they might initially appear.

Drama and Art Integration Strategies 10

A world without art would be a dreary place indeed. Art mirrors culture and society through beauty and creativity. The need to incorporate art and drama instruction into classrooms is increasingly important and should be regarded as a priority. Cultivating the talents of artistic students and encouraging other students to enhance their artistic abilities is crucial for integrating multimodal learning into all classrooms. Bringing art and drama activities into classrooms adds dimension and depth to the learning experience. The fun-filled and expressive strategies in this chapter can nurture talents that may one day produce the next Eugene O'Neil or Pablo Picasso!

Workshop Fair Festivals

The Workshop Fair Festival (Stix, 2004) is a strategy that allows students to make their way through different parts of a unit in groups, at their own pace, and in an exciting manner. The teacher-coach sets up the fair, and over a period of one or two days, the students are required to take part in activities at various multimodal, multilevel workstations—all of them content-based, intellectually challenging, and fun. The strategy works best if teacher-coaches are already familiar with classroom workstations, where they collect a variety of texts, manipulatives, and materials for student use. In the Workshop Fair Festival, the workstations differ in that they focus on specific skills, items, and procedures that become a cohesive whole and bring unity to the lesson. For example, students may be asked to make a rubbing of a leaf or take an impression of their fingerprint. They may be asked to form a coil pot or draw a caricature from a piece of literature.

Once the strategy has been explained to students, criteria must be agreed upon through negotiation with the teacher. Some criteria appropriate for this activity include working collaboratively as a group, respecting the materials, completing the task carefully, generating good notes throughout the process, noting the relevance of the workstation to the unit of study, and leaving the workstation in good condition for the next group.

To begin, the teacher-coach should decide on the number of activities that students will be required to work through. For each activity, the coach should prepare information sheets that outline the background for the material and the task each group must perform at each workstation. Next, a workstation for each activity is set up by pushing desks into clusters spaced comfortably around the room. The class should be divided into as many groups as there are activities.

At each station, the information sheet is posted and materials for completing the activity are made available. The teacher-coach may decide to provide students with the background information ahead of time. On the day of the simulation, each group takes its place at a workstation, where the students read the information sheet and complete the task. They should keep a journal of their experiences along the way. After finishing each assigned task, students should discuss what they have learned within their groups. Students are free to move from one workstation to another, as long as they are productively engaged. Enough materials should be set up so that at least two groups can work at a particular station at a time; some activities will take students longer to complete than others, and this way groups avoid unnecessary delays.

On the day of the simulation, the time each group spends at each station should be somewhat limited so that all of the groups can have the opportunity to visit each station. If necessary, the workshop can take place over the course of more than one day. When all of the groups have visited each of the workstations, the class comes together to discuss what all the tasks had in common, the problems that were encountered in each of the activities, how the material contributed to a better understanding of the unit, and what further information students need. The students should also reflect on how the information they covered affects their lives. As a writing assignment, the teacher-coach may ask students to choose the theme of one of the workstations as the subject of an essay and write about its relevance in modern society, its importance to our own lives, and how it contributes to the culture and civilization of the world.

The Workshop Fair Festival gets students actively involved in their learning. They discuss the content, manipulate materials, work together to achieve goals, and reflect on their experiences so that learning may be more meaningful and long-term. It's a fun way to approach units where several parts can be studied together. If it requires some additional preparation and imagination on the part of the teacher-coach, it's well worth it!

Classroom Application

In the language arts classroom, workstations could focus on specific poets or groups of poets; tasks could include writing poetry, revising a great poem, writing letters from one poet to another, crafting poems into lyrics with accompanying music, or even drawing visual representations of poems.

In social studies class, the Workshop Fair Festival can be used to make a specific historical period come alive. For instance, in a unit on ancient China, one workstation might ask students to read about and try their hands at calligraphy; another might ask them to do the same with pottery; a third could emphasize China's ancient paper-making methods, with students studying period drawings and placing the illustrations in the proper sequence; and so on.

In science class, small chemistry experiments can be set up at each workstation. The rotating groups must read about the importance of each experiment and its function and relevance to the unit of study, perform the experiment, and then note the outcomes and why the experiments worked the way they did. Alternatively, if the area of study is botany, workstations can be set up for different varieties of plants, with detailed information on each.

Amazing Fan Fold Designs

The Amazing Fan Fold Design strategy (Stix, 1994) adapts the methods of Yacov Agam, an Israeli artist whose work is well known at modern art museums such as New York City's Museum of Modern Art and Washington, D.C.'s Hirshhorn. Using Agam's technique, students compare and contrast two different subjects (e.g., two periods in history, two literary characters, or two scientific properties). The approach requires students to create visually appealing art that illustrates two different subjects on either side of a fold design. Students are required to work together, conduct adequate research, create the fold design, write descriptive paragraphs, and present their displays to the rest of the class. The reward for their hard work is a lasting piece of artwork that can be displayed either in the hallway or in the classroom for other students to enjoy throughout the year.

At the inception of the activity, it is helpful if the teacher-coach creates his own fold design, to serve as a model for the class. Using an example from a previous year's class is always a good idea too. In describing the fold design, the teacher tells the students they will be asked to choose two subjects. After conducting appropriate research at the classroom workstation, local library, or on the Internet, they should compare and contrast the material using a Venn diagram or T-chart. Working in pairs, the students discuss the material in depth before each student chooses a side of the fold design to illustrate, either by drawing a picture or creating a collage. The teacher-coach circulates from pair to pair, helping students transfer key concepts into pictorial form. The students will then create an amazing fold design by cutting their pictures into strips and attaching them to opposite views of the fan-folded cardstock. After creating the folds, students will be asked to write a concise, descriptive paragraph about their illustrations and what they represent. A title should be given to each fold design, and each pair of students should present its work before the entire class.

Once the class understands the task, the negotiable contracting of criteria can take place. Good research, suitable illustrations, interesting design and color, and descriptive paragraphs are some criteria that may be included. The teacher-coach fills out assessment charts for each student during the activity, and students may be asked to assess their classmates' work as well.

To begin construction, students should draw on paper, placed in a landscape position, that has lightly sketched vertical lines spaced one inch apart on the reverse side. The sections should be numbered one through nine. Students should also be given two pieces of cardstock, scored into sections one inch wide as well and attached by tape in the middle, on which to secure their pictures. The cardstock should be folded like a fan at the scored sections. When their pictures are complete, one student from each pair cuts his picture into nine equal sections according to the lines on the reverse side and fastens them to the cardstock on every fold facing from one view. The strips must be kept in their numbered sequence. The other student follows suit, but places the picture on the folds from the opposite view. When the work is finished, one picture should be viewable from one end of the design, and a completely different picture from the other end (see Figure 10.1). Before presenting their folds to the class, as in Figure 10.2, students should decide ahead of time which visual aspects to emphasize for comparison, and

Figure 10.1

Two Different Views of an Amazing Fan Fold Design: Rural vs. Urban Life in the 1800s

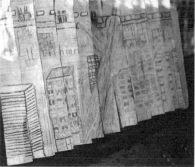

then take turns describing their finished artwork to the class. The teacher-coach may decide to offer a large poster board to each pair, placing their title, fan fold, and descriptions for display, as shown in Figure 10.2.

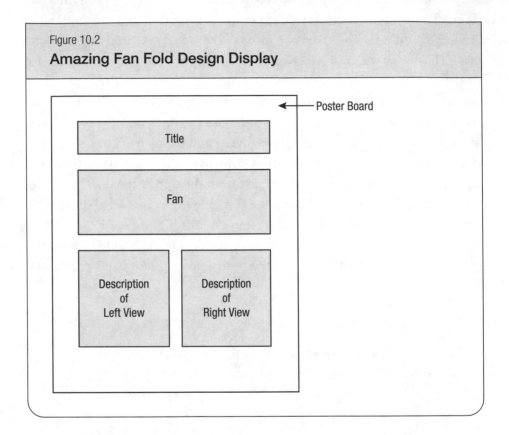

Figure 10.2
Amazing Fan Fold Design Display

As a reflection, students may be asked to describe the methods they applied when putting their pictures together; they may even do this as a journal entry in the voice of an artist. Students can also write comparison/contrast essays about the two illustrated subjects.

Classroom Application

This activity can be incorporated into just about any study. In language arts, the principal characters of a novel or a play can be compared, contrasted, examined, and illustrated. The same procedure can be applied to the settings of any literary work. Two different poems dealing with the same topic could serve as adequate subjects too.

In social studies, the strategy is particularly useful for before-and-after examinations: the South before and after the Civil War, Europe before and after World War II, and New York City before and after the 20th century are just a few possible examples. The activity can also be used to compare two historical figures.

In science class, students may be asked to compare and contrast two planets and illustrate them in a galactic splash of fascinating color. Other options could include comparing and contrasting two elements, two species of birds, or two types of flora.

Mystery Boxes

The Mystery Box strategy (Stix & Hrbek, 2001a) has students examine a topic in depth and create a representational artistic object, in the shape of a simple shoebox, with an accompanying written presentation on index cards. Students are then required to guess the topic that each of their classmates' boxes address by reading clues in the artwork and on the enclosed index cards. All the while, they work together and talk content, pool their information, and take part in an appealing, fun-filled, hands-on, creative presentation.

As in many of these creative exercises, it is helpful if the teacher has an example of a "mystery box" to model for students before the strategy begins. The teacher-coach explains to the class that they will be conducting research to write a piece on a particular person, character, book, scientific topic, or any other focus of the lesson. Once they have completed their research and shared their knowledge with group members, they will decorate shoeboxes that represent their topics. The illustrations should give subtle clues to the subject's identity, but never reveal it outright. Students can use drawings, photographs, charts, maps, flags, diagrams, or any tangible object that lends itself as a clue.

Students should divide the accompanying written work into four parts, attach them to four index cards, and place them in their shoeboxes. On the back of each index card should be written a word or two that, together with the words on the backs of other index cards, make up an entire quote that represents the subject. (For example, if the mystery subject is Paul Revere, the quote might be "The British are coming," with one word of that phrase written on the back of each card.) The bottom of the box should have the same quote, hidden by a flap; the inside of the lid to the box should reveal the subject's identity.

Once the activity has been described and explained, the class must decide on the criteria for assessment. These could include depth of research, well-written text, relevant decorations, and appealing artwork. Next, in whole-class format, students should brainstorm a list of questions that they want to answer in doing their research. They should recommend questions that they *have* to answer—those of the "who, what, when, where, why, and how" variety—as well as questions they would *like* to answer about a particular category in the content area (persons, birds, plant life, etc.). The questions may be charted on the board as a reference. Research should begin at the multimodal and multilevel workstation, and individual research should be conducted over the course of about a week.

The teacher divides the class into groups of four and then subdivides the groups into pairs. In their pairs, students decide what subject they would like to research from a list provided by the teacher. Each pair must select a different subject. The pair may conduct the research as one, but the students will write their essays and create their mystery boxes individually. The essays should be exactly four paragraphs long, and approximately one typed page in length. The paragraphs must be organized in sequential order, with clues to the sequencing (by using such terms as "First," "In the beginning," "Following," or "At the end"), and the subject should not be named. Student pairs discuss what they've found, scrutinize and edit each other's writing, and share suggestions for improvement. The teacher-coach circulates the room, giving guidance and helping students identify key concepts, write about them succinctly, and transfer that knowledge into pictorial representations.

Now the real work begins. Students must type their written reports using wide margins and an easy-to-read typeface, so that the individual paragraphs can be taped to 4- by 6-inch index cards. The teacher must instruct all students to use the same font and size, so that information can't be linked to any one student. Students should affix their paragraphs to the index cards and write their quote segments on the flip sides. Then each student acquires a shoebox and cuts a slit in the top before embarking upon the task of decorating it (see Figure 10.3). Three-dimensional objects may be attached to the top and sides of the box. The students must remember to include the quote on the bottom of the box and identify the mystery subject on the inside of the lid.

Figure 10.3
Mystery Boxes

The teacher-coach then has students count off *A, B, C,* and *D* within their groups. All *A*s and *C*s are placed in a "red" group, and all *B*s and *D*s are placed in a "blue" group, bringing their shoeboxes with them. Within the blue and red groups, the students jigsaw once more into groups of four, making sure that these subgroups don't contain more than one student from a given home-base group. In their subgroups, the students combine their index cards into one pile and shuffle them well. Now all the subgroups in the red group rotate to another table, still within their red group, and the blue group does the same. The mystery game is ready to begin.

A student picks a card from the top of the pile and reads it aloud. The group tries to match the paragraph to a box by noting clues from the decorations, pictures, or objects on each box. They then insert the index card through the top slot of the chosen box. The next student in the group chooses the next card and reads it, and the process is repeated until all the cards have been placed in the boxes. The students then open each box one at a time and read the cards inside, trying to place them in sequential order, from left to right. Once students think they know the identity of the subject, they flip the cards over to see if the quote is written in proper order. If so, they flip over the box and look on the bottom to see if the quote is a match. If the students believe they know the identity, they check the bottom of the lid to make certain. At this point, students may be asked to fill in a student assessment chart, critiquing the box they have just finished examining. The process is repeated for the other three mystery boxes. In the course of the activity, the teacher-coach circulates the room, filling in her own assessments based on the decided criteria.

The game is far from finished, however. Each group has only identified four subjects, and there are many more mystery boxes to examine! They remove all the cards from the boxes and shuffle them; the reds then rotate to new tables in their section, as do the blues, and the game begins anew. Together, students read and talk about the content, assess the artwork and writing of each essay and box, use analytical thinking to sequence written texts, and deduce the identity of the mystery boxes. The writing involved in this lesson demonstrates a purpose: namely, that all texts must be accurate, identifiable, well-written, comprehensive, and interesting. But more importantly, because they are writing for a purpose, students are teaching other students and "talking content."

As a follow-up assignment, students may be asked to expand their written research into a longer biography, feature, or exposé for a class newsletter or magazine. They may be asked to compare and contrast two of the subjects they examined other than their own, or to write an art review of one of the boxes they examined. The important thing is that there is a purpose to the writing, so students do not feel they are simply writing for the teacher.

The Mystery Box strategy encourages students to approach content from a novel perspective. "The projects were creative, so we had to be creative to do them," said Emily Chuk, a 7th grade student at Robert Wagner Middle School. "We had to be artistic and think, because lots of the time the answers weren't just in the book."

Classroom Application

The Mystery Box strategy can be adapted to any number of subjects, and it can be a fun, useful way to integrate art, writing, and research into lessons. Students leave the classroom with a better understanding of multiple subjects—as well as a souvenir from the activity!

In language arts, the strategy can be used to analyze the major characters in a novel.

In social studies, it can be used to examine various historical figures in depth, such as the men and women of the Revolutionary War period, female activists in the suffragist movement, or tycoons of the Gilded Age.

In science, teachers can adapt the strategy to examine different scientists, inventors, or concepts (e.g., diseases or food groups).

Slide Show Alive

Now that computers are a ubiquitous part of the educational environment, this Slide Show Alive strategy (Stix & Hrbek, 2001b) can be particularly motivating. Although it is possible to complete this activity using overhead transparencies, many students will jump at the chance to create computer-generated presentations that incorporate artwork, primary sources, music, voiceovers, and all the other features common to filmed documentaries. The idea is for each group to put together a presentation for the class—a documentary of sorts—using visuals and slides.

To activate prior knowledge, the teacher-coach should ask students if they have ever watched a documentary, such as those shown on the History Channel or PBS. The teacher should consider bringing in an example of a documentary for the class to watch for approximately 10 minutes. Before the viewing takes place, the teacher-coach should ask the following questions so that a meaty discussion can ensue afterward:

- "Describe in detail what you remember about the presentation."
- "In what ways were primary sources used?"
- "Explain in detail how voices were incorporated into segments set so long ago that the original participants are not available."

- "Describe the music, and the many ways it's used."
- "In what ways does the documentary reflect the time period it is discussing?"
- "Describe the logic that was used to sequence the pictures."
- "Generate a list of what you learned from this program."

Students will work in groups to create documentaries dramatizing a particular time or event in history, a novel or play, a scientific discovery, or anything else that lends itself to sequenced dramatization. They should be aware that the documentaries are stories, and that they should flow together in a way that makes sense. Of course, there should be multiple topics within the unit that can be assigned to the different groups. Together, the teacher-coach and students brainstorm a list of topics that they would like to see presented. Each group of four to six students will be assigned one topic to dramatize. They will conduct research, collect illustrations, and write text to match the images they choose for the presentation. They will also sequence the slides or transparencies into a narrative tapestry that appeals to viewers, lend voices to at least two of the principal personalities featured in the documentary, and present narration to accompany the drama. Each student will be responsible for some aspect of the presentation: For instance, two students can write the narration, one can write the introduction, one can write the conclusion, and two can dramatize the main characters through voiceovers and costumes. They can all be responsible for editing the speeches for accuracy, detail, fact, flow, grammar, and spelling. Of course, each student should take part in the presentation itself—no student gets a free pass!

Now that students understand the task before them, the criteria for assessment should be agreed upon. As in other strategies, students may also be asked to assess each other's work, so they should keep that in mind at this point. Some appropriate criteria include a captivating introduction, appropriate and appealing pictures and narration, pictures and narration that blend well together, a natural flow and sequence to the presentation, evidence of deep research, accurate and dramatic characterizations, and a conclusion that brings the story home and leaves the viewers with something to think about.

Once the groups have chosen or been assigned a topic, they should divide the work among themselves in such a way that everyone has research responsibilities and a role to play in the presentation. A checklist of responsibilities can be devised and distributed to help guide students through the activity. The teacher should set up some multimodal and multilevel workstations in the classroom for the purpose of initial research, but research outside the classroom should be encouraged.

When students have conducted their research and gathered primary sources, they come together in their groups to discuss what they have found and to assemble their photographs and illustrations into a narrative format. The teacher-coach circulates from one group to the next. Students should be reminded that their goal is to tell the story of their subjects. For each illustration that they decide to include in their slides, a brief outline or informative caption should be crafted for the narration. These do not yet need to be formal or final, but they should set students on the path to the completed narration. The illustrations should be put in the proper order; as the teacher-coach circulates from group to group, he should provide feedback and sign off on the sequencing before the next step takes place. Once everyone has been given the OK by the teacher, students can begin writing the formal narration based on their outlines or captions.

As they put their presentations together, groups should decide which two of the figures in the collected photographs should "come alive." Of course, if students want to give more than two characters the breath of life, they should not be discouraged, but two should be the minimum required. When the slides for the chosen figures come up during the presentation, the students assigned to be the voices act out their roles. The students should be encouraged to dress up for this whenever possible. These students are also responsible for obtaining accurate quotations that can be directly attributed to the personalities. If they can't find any, and that's always a possibility, the students may try their hands at writing historical fiction instead. Students should be encouraged to have fun with the activity by acting out the part with dramatic gestures and voice projection.

Finally, captions should be created for each slide. Once the narrations are written and edited, and the illustrations are finalized and put in order, students must decide whether to transfer their visuals to transparencies or scan them into a computer program such as PowerPoint. (Of course, illustrations or photographs that have been downloaded from the Internet won't need to be scanned.) Students may decide to add background music or other voiceovers, and may even ask their parents or friends to record additional voices. In their groups, they should rehearse their presentations. It is preferable that they memorize their portion of the narration, but if they can't, they may write key words on index cards. The teacher-coach must emphasize that the one thing they must avoid is reading directly from their formal narrations; for this reason, the practice session is imperative. There is nothing more disheartening than watching a student with head bowed low reading her speech. In some cases, the teacher may decide that groups should rehearse their documentaries for other groups before getting up in front of the whole class. Of course, the teacher-coach circulates during the rehearsals, providing feedback, direction, praise, and guidance.

After each group presents its slide show, the rest of the students should fill out their peer assessment charts based on the criteria determined earlier. The teacher-coach also conducts an assessment at this point. Enough time should be allowed for questions and answers after each presentation; this offers each group an opportunity to clarify or expand on information.

As a postexercise, students may be asked to reflect on the activity in a journal entry by posing and answering an open-ended question. Alternatively, they may be asked to watch and write a review of a real documentary, addressing questions that the teacher may pose ahead of time. Perhaps they will be asked to create a year-end documentary on their own, featuring some important aspect of the year's curriculum. When students assemble again after the presentations, they may be asked to describe the top two things they learned from the documentaries. Using the active listening strategy, the teacher-coach may chart the results on the board.

The Slide Show Alive strategy is inherently motivating, as it taps many different talents, including speaking skills, writing, acting, illustrating, and editing. Students work together, making decisions, talking content, writing for purpose, critiquing materials, sequencing information, and presenting their masterpieces. They must cooperate and think creatively to complete the assignment, and everyone has a role to play.

Classroom Application

In language arts class, this strategy can be used for novels, with each group presenting a section of the work, bringing in information about the author and the world at the time the book was written. Alternatively, individual authors or poets can be profiled.

In social studies, students can make slide shows in conjunction with a lesson on the fall of Adolf Hitler, Julius Caesar, or even Richard Nixon.

This approach can be applied to the science classroom, too, where prominent scientists or animal species can be profiled. One way of generating ideas for subjects is to have students brainstorm a list of related topics within a unit and then choose the subjects suitable for the slide shows. Students feel a sense of ownership when they are part of the decision-making process, and they will feel it all the more after presenting their own special work.

Site Plan Design

The Site Plan Design (Stix, 1993) requires that students recreate a specific historical period using topography. Contour maps, together with special shapes cut to scale that present a bird's-eye view of the featured area, are essential for this activity. Students design colonial settlements using cut-outs of homes, farmlands, fortresses, outhouses, wells, houses of worship, and so on, placing them logically on a landscape. (This activity is described in greater detail in Chapter 5.)

Classroom Application

In language arts, students can recreate Medieval Paris when reading Victor Hugo's *The Hunchback of Notre Dame,* or Victorian London to follow the plot of Charles Dickens's *Oliver Twist.*

Social studies can use this strategy when studying such topics as ancient civilizations, the Middle Ages, the growth of Greek nation-states, 18th century mill towns, or antebellum Southern plantations.

Science teachers will find the strategy a challenging way to study topography, geology, strata, tectonics, and volcanic turbulence.

Playlets

William Shakespeare once observed, "All the world's a stage, and all the men and women merely players." True, but we also like a good performance, and being part of one can be more fun than simply sitting in the audience. So, if teachers agree with Jerome Kern that "There's no business like show business," they should try the Playlets strategy in their classrooms. This activity allows students to explore their writing, staging, and acting talents in the context of the subject they are studying. Writing and performing mini-plays, or playlets, is a hands-on activity that encourages the creative abilities, cooperative instincts, and performance skills of all students involved. Different groups write their own dialogue and produce playlets of interviews, puppet shows, jury trials, musicals, poetry readings, or any other type of performance. The key is to incorporate factual information within the setting of an entertaining show that the whole class can enjoy.

To begin, the teacher-coach asks cooperative groups to brainstorm a list of the types of performances they are familiar with, along with some characteristics of each. Using the active listening strategy, the teacher charts the various responses. When the list is exhausted, each group is assigned a particular genre to study further. Using a web design, students should chart what they have seen on TV, in the movies, or at the theater, drawing connections to the type of performance they are studying. For homework, each student conducts further research and reports to the group the next day.

Next, the teacher-coach assigns, or allows each group to choose, a topic related to the overall unit for which they will write enough designated roles so that everyone can take part. The coach tells the students that they will perform their scripts for the rest of the class. They will bring props, wear costumes, and enter into the full spirit of the role, but what they demonstrate in their performances must be accurate and reflect their research skills and scholarship.

Once the topics are assigned, groups should choose the format they would like to use for their performances. This does not necessarily have to be the format they researched for homework; the groups may choose whatever format they find most comfortable and suitable to their objectives. Each group member is responsible for researching some part of the topic and sharing that information with the group before the script is written. The important factor at this point is total harmony, as it would be most discouraging for all concerned if there were discord during the exercise. For instance, if two members of a group would not feel comfortable singing or doing a dance routine, the group should not choose to put on a musical.

As part of the preparation for the activity, the class should discuss what makes good dialogue. In whole-class format, the teacher-coach elicits relevant responses and charts them on the board. Engaging, succinct, clear, dramatic, grammatical, accurate, interesting, and informative are all potential criteria for dialogue, for performances, criteria might include strong voice projection, clear enunciation, and appropriate gestures. When the criteria are settled, students may be asked to make up assessment charts that they will use to critique each other's performances.

And now the playwriting begins! Students incorporate their research into meaningful dialogue, set the scene, and decide on props and costumes. Of course, rehearsal is paramount, so the teacher-coach should allow time for students to practice their playlets before the day of the performance. The props should be brought in for the rehearsal, so that they are not forgotten at home on the day the curtain rises. All the while, the teacher-coach rotates from group to group, providing assistance and making certain that all students keep to the schedule. If time permits, groups can exchange scripts and offer constructive ideas that might help smooth the rough edges before the performance.

When it is finally showtime, students should have their assessment charts handy to review the work of other groups. After each group performs, students in the other groups make notes and fill in their charts. The teacher-coach also assesses the performances based on the agreed-upon criteria. We recommend that the first group make an initial two-minute run, which can be critiqued by everyone, before they actually stage their performance for assessment. This form of modeling is extremely helpful to the rest of the class. When all the performances have taken place, the class should be asked to reflect on what they learned, what they would do differently if they did this again, and what they liked or disliked about the simulation. Many of the students may find they have an affinity for performing they did not know they had!

Students have talked content throughout this simulation, and now is a perfect time to incorporate a writing assignment. Teacher-coaches can ask students to put themselves in the role of theater reviewers, with each student choosing one of the performances and reviewing it for a classroom "Theater and the Arts" newsletter. Of course, the elements of a good review should be examined ahead of time. The objective is to make this exercise a learning experience, a forum for exchanging ideas and commentaries, not for putting classmates down.

Classroom Application

The Playlets strategy is useful in a variety of subject areas. Because students are asked to write their own dialogue, applicability of this strategy to the language arts classroom is a given. Teachers could ask students to imagine and illustrate what occurs "behind the scenes" of the action in a book. For instance, when studying Kate Chopin's "The Story of an Hour," students may be asked to write playlets illustrating what the husband had been doing while his wife received the news of his "death." Alternatively, playlets could focus on an author's life during its different stages.

In social studies, the strategy can be used to illustrate different historical periods or personages. The class can stage a series about Socrates, for example, with each group creating a playlet that deals with one specific segment or event of his life.

In science, this strategy could be used when studying vaccines, with each group performing a playlet on the discovery of cures for smallpox, measles, diphtheria, and polio. Or students can stage the circulation process, taking on the roles of red blood cells, white blood cells, and all the other components of blood!

Museum Scavenger Hunt

The Museum Scavenger Hunt strategy (Stix & Hrbek, 2001b) brings into play two different activities that engage students: finding visuals that illustrate items related to the subject being studied, and writing poems that describe the items. The ultimate goal of both activities is to identify each item as it relates to the topic at hand.

To begin, the teacher-coach asks students to create a web that describes certain "artifacts" representing the topic. There are no limitations on the subjects that may be used for this activity. For instance, if the students are reading Charles Dickens's *David Copperfield*, they may consider different objects unique to Victorian England that are described in the novel. Some of the items may be related, and others may not. Students may even come up with items that are not mentioned in the book. They should make their webs as comprehensive as possible, as they will be embarking on a "scavenger hunt" to locate photographs and illustrations of these items for an exhibit.

In their cooperative groups, the teacher-coach should choose a type of poem—such as a limerick, cinquain, or haiku—and ask students if they are familiar with it. An example of the poetic format should be distributed for examination; working in pairs within their groups, students then study the structure and rhyme scheme. If some students have an aversion to poetry they may choose to write prose.

The teacher explains to the class that they will be hunting for photographs and illustrations of selected artifacts from their webs and writing poetry or prose to describe them. The number of artifacts may vary, depending on how much the teacher-coach wants the students to cover. The teacher models the activity, preparing beforehand a few photographs of appropriate items, and calls on a pair of students to read a prewritten poem. The class helps the pair match the correct artifact to the descriptive poem.

Now that they understand what is expected of them, the teacher-coach and students can create the criteria for assessment together. Criteria typically focus on the poem and may require that it describe the photo accurately; provide the correct historical, literary, or scientific background; and have a good rhyming, prose, or pattern design. The teacher-coach should caution students that providing factual, detailed information about an object sometimes necessitates sacrificing the poetic rhythm and balance that are expected of well-written poems. The teacher-coach should also make it clear that great poets are great precisely because they *don't* sacrifice rhythm and balance for accuracy.

Students may be asked to download and print photos off the Internet or photocopy illustrations in reference books that reflect their artifacts. A pair may choose to draw its own illustration of an item, or even build a three-dimensional model. Each pair of students is asked to write description cards for the artifacts using their chosen form (whether poetry or prose). In their pairs, students choose items of major importance that are of particular interest to them and begin to conduct their research. Once they have photocopied their illustrations, they may write their descriptions individually. When they come to class with their artifacts ready for display, the students in each pair will review one another's work. Once their work is ready, the teacher-coach rotates from pair to pair, providing assistance that might be required. The description cards are photocopied so that each pair receives a set of all of them. Students post their visuals randomly around the room. If time permits, pairs can review other pairs' poems or prose and suggest improvements.

Now the fun begins. In their pairs, students must match the description cards to the illustrations. They count off by *A*s and *B*s, with the *A*s reading a certain number of lines and the *B*s reading the rest. Again, teachers should remember that the rhyme and rhythm must sometimes be sacrificed for there to be a thorough and factual description of the object. A modification of this strategy is for the pairs to read their descriptions in front of the class, with the students alternating lines; the class will then have to match the descriptions to the pictures.

The teacher-coach assesses the students' work according to the negotiated criteria. As a postactivity, students are asked what they learned from the scavenger hunt. Using active listening, the coach charts the responses by category, but doesn't label the categories. When all responses have been charted, the teacher-coach asks students to provide the labels for the categories. They should record the findings in their notes.

Classroom Application

The Museum Scavenger Hunt strategy can be used across the curriculum. In language arts, items noted in a given novel can be the subject of the scavenger hunt, and the description cards can incorporate specifics from the story; just imagine creating a Museum Scavenger Hunt depicting one of Sir Arthur Conan Doyle's Sherlock Holmes stories. Alternatively, when studying the literature of a particular time period, students may be asked to research the lives of several authors and provide "artifacts" with which the authors are identified. The pictures can be left around the room until the unit is complete, students can remain immersed in the time period being studied, and the information can more readily move from short- to long-term memory.

In social studies class, the strategy is particularly useful for helping students get a better sense of different world cultures past and present. Examining "artifacts" from ancient Greek, Roman, or Chinese civilizations brings a greater understanding of the time period.

In science, this activity can be used for a unit on ancient life forms. Pictures of fossils representing different categories of animals or plants are well suited to descriptive writing. Imagine what the class can do with dinosaurs, early mammals, or today's endangered species.

Cooperative Time Lines

Time is measured in seconds, minutes, hours, days, weeks, months, years, centuries, and millennia. We feel time as we grow old, but we can never actually see it. When students create time lines, they are creating a visual representation of time that endows its passage with a measure of reality. Everyone has probably seen a time line at some point, but not everyone has taken part in the challenging activity of actually constructing one.

Time lines can help students visualize major events in history that overlap or occur simultaneously by splicing them together in an ornate tapestry that relates the events in sequence. By creating their own time lines, students engage in an art activity that uses their inquiry and cooperative skills. The students work together, conduct research, and combine their work into one overall classroom time line that they can refer to throughout the unit.

The Cooperative Time Lines strategy (Stix, 1994) is ideal for units in which major developments take place over the course of a specified time period. To begin the lesson, a teacher-coach asks students to consider what they did over the course of an hour that morning (e.g. spanning from 6:00–7:00 a.m.). On paper, students draw a five-inch time line marked by 15-minute intervals, one inch apart. Along the line, they fill in all that they did, using notches to attach their information to the correct time. Figure 10.4 shows an example of the type of information the students might jot down.

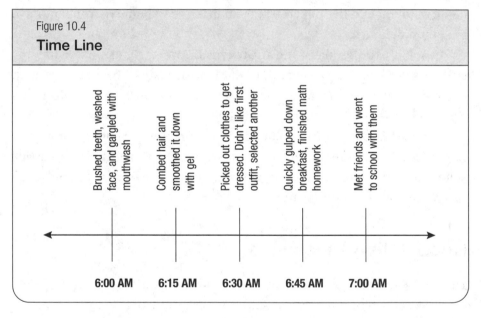

Figure 10.4
Time Line

In cooperative groups, the students place their individual time lines one on top of the other to merge them, aligning the notches, and discuss what they notice (e.g., Why did one person take much longer brushing his teeth than everyone else? For what reasons did one person eat breakfast before getting dressed?). After discussing the time lines, students should make a list of conclusions that can be shared with the whole class using the active listening strategy.

Now that students have had a chance to understand the way activities unfold in individual lives during the same time periods, they should be asked to stand around the perimeter of the room. The teacher-coach places the subject cards, one for each group, on each of the group tables. The teacher describes the subject of each card in a way that makes it sound appealing. The subjects should represent a topic that changed over time and that has a rich history (for instance, when studying the conquest of the Americas, the subject cards could include the names of the famous explorers or the countries involved). After reading all the cards and briefly describing each, the coach should ask for volunteers to research each subject, forming new groups. It is best if there are no more than four students for each cooperative group, but if one topic seems to be very popular, including it twice is fine if there is enough information to be uncovered. If there are not enough volunteers, the teacher may have to shuffle students around so that groups do not have more than four students each.

Now that they have their topics, students should brainstorm a list of questions they would like answered in their groups. For example, if the subjects are the nations involved in the conquest of the Americas, questions for each country might include the following: Who were the most famous explorers from this nation? What areas did they subjugate? For what reasons did the explorers embark on these journeys? In what ways did they succeed or fail in their explorations?

In whole-class format, the teacher-coach then elicits the questions one at a time from each group using active listening, and records the responses on the board. Next, groups decide who will be responsible for which portions of the research. The work should be shared equitably. In the above example, each student may be assigned a different explorer to research. Alternatively, one person might be responsible for researching the country's military commanders, one might research the economy, one might examine the levels of society, and one might examine conflicts the country had with other nations. Once the jobs are assigned, a "contract" that reflects each student's role should be completed. The teacher-coach may even decide to provide students with a checklist of all the things they need to do to complete the work, which they can refer to along the way.

The negotiable contracting of criteria can take place once the activity is clearly explained to the class. Some criteria for assessment appropriate to this strategy could include the following: chronologically ordered information, appealingly presented time line, in-depth and descriptive content, accurate information, and excellent photographic or illustrative material.

In conducting their research, students should collect pictures, charts, graphs, maps, diagrams, and other visual materials to include as part of the time line. They may even decide to draw their own illustrations, and they should be encouraged to make their time lines as aesthetically appealing as possible. Because the group time lines will later be merged into a single, whole-class time line, students should make photocopies of all their visuals.

As they proceed through their research, students should keep a journal of notes and illustrations, which can be collected or reviewed by the teacher-coach along the way. All the while, the coach circulates from group to group, using appropriate coaching skills and giving assistance.

In class, students should be given the opportunity to draft their group time lines on basic letter paper. The groups and the teacher-coach can provide feedback on the drafts; for homework, students should complete their part of the research. Once students have completed their research, they are asked to highlight the most important events in their notes, rewrite them in brief but clear language, and make note of the exact date or time span when they occurred. At first, they place all of this information on their group time line, using a legal-size piece of paper. (Every group's time line should be the same size, with the same number of intervals; this integrates a bit of mathematics into the lesson.) The students then transfer their illustrations and captions to 3- to 5-inch index cards that are attached to their own standard-sized time line, which should be drawn on wrapping paper or newsprint, with each group using a different colored marker to write in its information.

Once the groups have finished placing their time lines on the larger paper, they should all be able to be viewed simultaneously along an entire stretch of classroom wall. Because each group was given the same span within which to work, the events on the sheets of paper should coalesce. As in other strategies, students are writing for purpose. The information written on the time line becomes a catalyst for students to talk and compare content. They can describe in detail what happened during their time period, or they can compare it to another group's information. Students engaged in active listening should be taking notes or filling in an information chart during the presentations, but any assessment should be based on the criteria decided on earlier.

The lesson could end there, but that would limit the fun. Students are now asked to present their time lines to the class. This can be achieved in two ways: each group can get up and describe its time line from beginning to end, with group members taking turns speaking; or the time lines can be broken down into time segments, and one person from each group can describe what occurred during that interval of time for her group's topic.

As a follow-up activity, the whole class can create time lines based on current events or world crises. Students can also be asked to periodically bring in examples of time lines they may find in newspapers, magazines, or other media. But writing is key: For example, students may be asked to write essays discussing two events that took place at the same time in different places, describing in detail what they had in common and how they influenced each other. Alternatively, they may be asked to write a feature article or news report for the TV news that describes the events taking place at that instant in different parts of the world. Giving students a purpose for their writing adds an element of reality and motivates them to do the best they can and to be creative and engaging in their writing.

Classroom Application

The Cooperative Time Lines strategy can be adapted to any number of lessons. In language arts class, time lines can reflect the action of long, sprawling novels like Leo Tolstoy's *War and Peace,* or they can focus on a specific group of famous authors, such as African American writers. Time lines can also be used to merge history and literature by noting the action in a book alongside the real-world activity taking place at the time the book is set. This approach works particularly well for historical fiction, such as Victor Hugo's *Les Misérables* or Ernest Hemingway's *A Farewell to Arms.*

The example of exploration, as mentioned previously, is appropriate for the social studies classroom. Cooperative Time Lines can also be used to compare ancient civilizations where different cultures existed simultaneously.

In science class, time lines can be used to examine the theory of evolution; there could be one subject card each for Homo, Homo Habilis, Homo Erectus, Neanderthal, Cro-Magnon, and Homo Sapiens. (Students are always surprised to discover that many of our predecessors actually lived for a short while simultaneously, perhaps even in adjoining environments.) Just imagine the illustrations students may come up with!

11 The Nine Steps of Project-Based Learning

Whether students work individually, in pairs, or in groups, having them design something from scratch taps their creative abilities. When using the project-based learning strategy, it is almost guaranteed that the endeavor will be interdisciplinary. The teacher's role is to serve as coach, guiding students to use a variety of resources, employ a strategy that is fun and motivating, and uncover content with depth and breadth.

If we examine project-based learning in the most general way, we can break it down into the following nine steps (of course, teacher-coaches should modify the steps accordingly to suit the task and the students):

1. The teacher-coach **sets the stage for students with real-life samples** of the projects they will be doing.

2. Students **take on the role of project designers,** possibly establishing a forum for display or competition.

3. Students **discuss and accumulate the background information** needed for their designs.

4. The teacher-coach and students **negotiate the criteria for evaluating the projects.**

5. Students **accumulate the materials** necessary for the project.

6. Students **create their projects**.

7. Students **prepare to present their projects.**

8. Students **present their projects.**

9. Students **reflect on the process and evaluate the projects** based on the criteria established in Step 4.

Now let's examine how these nine steps apply to a real-life project.

Project-Based Learning Example:
The Roman Arch Bridge Activity

When studying transportation and its effects on the economy of Ancient Rome, students in Mr. Jordan's 9th grade social studies class honed in on the Roman invention of the arch bridge. Realizing the depth and breadth of the innovation, Mr. Jordan decided that the students should role-play Roman engineers and design their own Roman arch bridges using paper materials.

Step 1: Setting the Stage with Real-Life Examples

With the help of the school's science teacher, Mr. Jordan set the stage for his students to study the arch bridge. He explained that the major advantage of the construction was that it had a large passage for vessels to pass through. The Roman transportation system was a key priority for continuous military campaigns, as well as for the trade that was carried to all corners of the empire. Mr. Jordan showed the students different types of bridges, demonstrating the differences between the arch bridge and the primitive structures that existed prior to its invention.

Step 2: Taking on the Role of Project Designers

Having his goal in mind, Mr. Jordan assigned the students their roles as engineers for Roman firms. He explained that they were commissioned by the emperor, but had to use paper materials for their model constructions. Each group of two to three students was to be a firm competing with other groups to build a bridge that would meet predetermined specifications and be subjected to heavy weight.

Step 3: Discussing and Accumulating Necessary Background Information

Students conducted research on the arch bridge and learned that the center keystone was critical to distributing weight evenly to each side. They saw the advantage of the Roman arch bridge over post-and-lintel constructions, which did not offer as much clearance for whatever passed beneath. The even distribution of weight created by an arch bridge's keystone made the structure more reliable, adding a degree of stability and security.

Mr. Jordan and his students determined the parameters of the construction, setting strictly defined limits to the length of the bridge and the roadway above.

Step 4: Negotiating the Criteria for Evaluation

Mr. Jordan and his students decided that the projects should be assessed by asking the following questions:

- Did the group design and construct a bridge that employed the Roman arch concept?
- Did the "engineers" try to keep their expenditures low?
- Did the bridge support the weight that was placed upon it?

Once the criteria were clearly defined, the students realized that they might have to be modified in the future.

Step 5: Accumulating the Necessary Materials

The students decided that they would use paper or soft balsa wood and glue or tape to make their arch bridges. Mr. Jordan told them that any material they needed would have to be purchased at a mock store, and they were expected to keep track of their expenditures on an expense sheet. For example, a sheet of paper, representing stone, "cost" $1,000; a tablespoon of glue, representing cement, "cost" $2,000. Mr. Jordan reminded students that construction commodities were very expensive in Ancient Rome. Students decided that the bridge that withstood the most weight and was most cost-effective would win.

Step 6: Creating the Project

Students in each group worked on preliminary sketches and graphic organizers until they decided on a final design. During this stage, Mr. Jordan served as coach, moving from group to group to guide the students' work. As he did so, he asked himself the following COACHing questions (reflective of the COACH Model in Chapter 3):

- Do the students have a *clear* understanding of the task?
- Does each student have *ownership* of her role within the group?
- Are the students *attentive* and working together cooperatively?
- Are the resources that students use geared to their *comprehensive* level of understanding?
- Are any groups stumbling in a way that is blocking their work due to *heightened* emotions?

Mr. Jordan's role as coach obtained a clarity of purpose throughout this process. Prompted by the COACHing questions and the GOPER Model, the students used their own intellects to solve problems while attaining a higher level of learning.

Step 7: Preparing to Present the Project

The students in each group prepared for the final stages, discussing whether or not the presentations needed to be rehearsed, or whether display cards had to be written. They also made note of the following:

- Who designed and built the arch bridge
- The cost expended on materials
- What made their design aesthetically appealing
- What they thought was unique about their design
- What made their arch bridge strong enough to hold the weight that was placed on it

Step 8: Presenting the Project

During this stage, students become aware of the ways their presentations meet the criteria of assessment. The teacher-coach observes how engaged they are in presenting their projects. Each group in Mr. Jordan's class showcased its arch bridge to the class, explaining how the design was achieved. Testing one bridge at a time, weight was placed on top of it, to determine how much stress the bridge could bear without collapsing. Not one student was absent on the day of the competition.

Step 9: Reflecting on the Process and Evaluating the Process

In this simulation, the students discussed what they enjoyed about working in pairs or small groups, and how one student's idea would spawn another student's idea. They discussed what they liked about the materials and what they found to be frustrating. Students shared their reflections to note what they had in common and what was special to each pair or to each individual personally. They reviewed the criteria of assessment and discussed how well they met them.

• • •

The chart in the Appendix can serve as an example, and also as a catalyst, for teachers to creatively brainstorm ways to include project-based learning using the workshop model within their curricula. Note that the chart is brief, thus allowing teachers to generate their own ideas for projects that would be applicable to their own areas of specialization.

Section Summary

When students practice decision making and deductive reasoning and are exposed to examples from real life, they are able to expand their skills, evaluate their options, and think critically. The activities in this section help students visualize how events actually unfold by having students conduct research, discuss and write about the material, collect or draw illustrations, and reflect on their work. Students learn from each other by analyzing and synthesizing material, reinforcing main points, and moving information from short- to long-term memory. Most importantly, students "talk content" and write for a purpose, because their work is often presented in front of their peers. We hope that you will use these hands-on, interactive strategies to motivate and engage your students, and to foster an environment that makes learning fun.

Conclusion

This book brings educators a coaching system that has garnered success in the worlds of sports and business. We feel it is an idea whose time has come. Putting a coaching system into place is a major change, but as we well know, without change there is no progress. We caution educators that learning the techniques of coaching and creating coaching schools are not quick fixes; these are not simple ideas that can be taught in one day. Coaching is an ongoing process that requires teachers to meet weekly to discuss their coaching skills and classroom issues, and to determine ways to resolve conflicts as well as enhance instruction. It requires strategies to be tested and reflected upon, and teachers to train students on using coaching techniques with their peers. As your school becomes a coaching environment, your students' motivation and engagement will increase and their behavioral issues will decrease, because coaching is a catalyst for stronger self-image and higher achievement.

—Andi and Frank

Appendix

Examples of
Project-Based Assignments

MATH/TECHNOLOGY

Strategies	Ancient Times	World	United States
Bridges	• Primitive bridges • Post-and-lintel bridges • Roman arch bridges	• Medieval drawbridges • London Bridge • The Venetian Bridge of Sighs	• Brooklyn Bridge • The Mississippi River Bridge • The Golden Gate Bridge
Graphic Time Lines	• The Ming Dynasty • The Mogul Empire • The spread of Islam	• The Meiji Restoration • The life of Leonardo Da Vinci • The life of Peter the Great	• The Civil War • Westward expansion • The New Deal era
Map Designs	• The campaigns of Alexander the Great • The battles of Julius Caesar • Trade routes of the Incas	• The conquests of Genghis Khan • Burton's exploration of Africa • The Viking voyages	• The Oregon Trail • Explorations of Lewis & Clark • Powell's exploration of the Grand Canyon
Site Plan Designs	• Machu Picchu • The Greek Acropolis • An Egyptian peasant community	• A medieval manor • China's Forbidden City • Abbasid Circular City of Baghdad	• A colonial settlement • An antebellum Southern plantation • A post–Civil War frontier army fort
Architectural Structures	• An Egyptian pyramid • The Athenian Acropolis • The Roman Pantheon	• A Gothic cathedral • A Byzantine hippodrome • The Globe Theatre	• Fort Sumter • Monticello • The Port of New York at Ellis Island

WRITTEN AND PICTORAL ARTS

Strategies	Ancient Times	World	United States
Broadsides/Pamphlets	• Recruitment for the Athenian phalanx • Recruitment for the slave uprising of Spartacus • Announcement of the unification of China	• Recruitment for the Crusades • Peasant revolt in England in 1381 • Condemnations of medieval anti-Semitism	• Recruitment for the Union Army • Call to ignore the Fugitive Slaves Act • Endorsement of women's suffrage
Travel Brochures	• Ancient Babylon • The Nile during the Dynastic Period • Rome at the height of empire	• The Islamic world during the Ummayad Dynasty • Ancient African kingdoms (Shaka Zulu) • The Holy Roman Empire	• Battlefields of the War of Independence • California during the Gold Rush • The Santa Fe Trail
Journals of Historical Figures	• King Leonidas at Thermopylae • Nefertiti • A Roman slave	• Michelangelo • Catherine the Great • A Samurai warrior	• Harriet Tubman • A Cheyenne warrior • A Pilgrim
Historical Newspapers	• The Assyrian Empire • Ancient Egypt • The Aztec Empire	• Dynastic China • The Muromachi Period in Japan • The Byzantine Empire	• Colonial times • The 1960s • The War of 1812
Photographic Essays	• Greek architectural nomenclature • Egyptian pottery • The greatest of Rome's emperors	• St. Peter's Cathedral • The Great Potato Famine • Statues of Michelangelo	• Child labor in the early 1900s • The Robber Barons • Great American Indian chiefs
Short Stories or Story Books	• A woman's role in Athenian society • The daily life of an Egyptian Pharaoh • The experiences of a Greek rower at Salamis	• A medieval knight's quest for the Holy Grail • The life of the daughter of Tsar Nicholas and Tsarina Alexandra • The lives of the Soong sisters	• The life of Eleanor Roosevelt • The life of Rosa Parks • The experiences of a female black slave

FINE ARTS

Strategies	Ancient Times	World	United States
Classroom Museums	• Ancient Egypt • The city-states of ancient Greece • Mesoamerica	• The Ummayad Dynasty • The Muromachi Period in Japan • Mogul India	• American Indian tribes • Colonial times • The Asian-American experience
Fan Fold Designs	• The West vs. the East • Hunters vs. farmers • Monotheism vs. paganism	• Europe before and after the Black Death • The Middle East before and after the Ottoman Empire • Dynastic vs. Communist China	• Pre– and post–Civil War society • Urban vs. rural life • 19th vs. 20th century women
Political Cartoons	• The Jewish diaspora • The end of the Roman Republic • The Delian League	• Events of the Reformation • The Dark Ages • Dynastic China	• The War of Independence • The Civil War • The Civil Rights Movement
Re-creations	• Masada • A Greek city-state • A Mesoamerican village	• Medieval Paris • Baghdad during the Abassid Dynasty • The world of Renaissance Florence	• San Francisco during the Gold Rush • New York during the Gilded Age • Washington, D.C., during the Civil War
Tableaus (stained-glass windows, mosaics)	• Hellenistic mosaics • Roman glass • Egyptian glass beads and amulets	• Byzantine mosaics • Rose windows • Galileo's telescope lenses	• Tiffany glass • Corning Glass Works • Chihuly's *Fiori di Como*

SPOKEN ART

Strategies	Ancient Times	World	United States
Guided Tours	• Egypt under the Rameses • The Persian Empire of Cyrus • The Rome of Augustus	• The Silk Road • Marco Polo's travels • India under the Raj	• The colonies • The Western frontier • The country during the Great Depression

Interviews	• Genghis Khan • Themistocles • Akbar	• Nelson Mandela • Mikhai Gorbachev • Archduke Franz Ferdinand	• Charles Lindbergh • John Wilkes Booth • Elizabeth Blackwell
Plays	• The assassination of Julius Caesar • The trial of Alcibiades • The trial of Socrates	• The trial of Joan of Arc • Martin Luther at the Diet of Worms • King John's signing of the Magna Carta	• The drafting of the Declaration of Independence • The trial of Andrew Johnson • The McCarthy hearings
Poem and Prose Read-Alouds	• The Olympian Gods and Goddesses • Remus and Romulus • The Epic of Gilgamesh	• Viking warriors • The life of Richard the Lion-hearted • The rule of Charlemagne	• The life of Sitting Bull • William Travis at the Alamo • Custer at Little Big Horn
Music	• The songs of ancient Persia • Ancient Greek music • Garba dance songs of North India	• Chants of the Benedictine monks • Troubadour songs of the Renaissance • Ude dance songs of the Urhobo	• The music of the Jazz Age • Songs of the Civil War era • Appalachian folk songs
Speeches	• Hannibal announces his hatred of Rome • Spartans boast of military prowess • Emperor Wu announces the extension of the Chinese empire	• Reformers attack the sale of indulgences • English barons oppose King John • Empress Theodora stands up to rebels	• Democratic-Republicans decree their opposition to the Federalists • Republicans attack the New Deal • American Indians plea for justice
TV News Stories	• Hannibal's crossing of the Alps • Nebuchadnezzar's invasion of Judea • The Vandal sack of Rome	• The Crusades • Genghis Khan's conquering of the Mongols • The Middle Passage	• The massacre at Little Big Horn • The building of the Panama Canal • The assassination of John F. Kennedy

Bibliography

Annis, L. (1983). The processes and effects of peer tutoring. *Human Learning, 2,* 39–47.

Bargh, J., & Schul, Y. (1980). On the cognitive benefits of teaching. *Journal of Educational Psychology, 72,* 593–604.

Benware, C. A., & Deci, E. L. (1984). Quality of learning with an active versus passive motivational set. *American Educational Research Journal, 21*(4), 755–765.

Bonwell, C. C., & Eison, J. A. (1991). *Active learning: Creating excitement in the classroom.* Washington, DC: George Washington University.

Carlson, R. (2003). *Taming your gremlin: A surprisingly simple method for getting out of your own way.* New York: HarperCollins.

Cashin, W. E. (1985). *Improving lectures.* (Report No. 14). Manhattan, KS: Center for Faculty Evaluation and Development, Kansas State University.

CoachPeople Training. (2003). *Distinction between coaching and other professions.* Bedminster, PA: Author.

CoachWorks International. (1995). *The coaching clinic: Strategic corporate coaching skills for managers, leaders, and coaches.* Dallas, TX: Author.

Conway, M. A., Cohen, G., & Stanhope, N. (1991). On the very long-term memory of knowledge acquired through formal education: Twelve years of cognitive psychology. *Journal of Experimental Psychology, 120,* 395–408.

Crane, T. (2002). *The heart of coaching: Using transformational coaching to create a high-performance culture.* San Diego, CA: FTA Press.

Durling, R., & Shick, C. (1976). Concept attainment by peers and individuals as a function of vocalization. *Journal of Educational Psychology, 68*(1), 83–91.

Dutton, G. (1997, February). Executive coaches call the plays. *Management Review,* 39–43.

Elder, L., & Paul, R. (2002). *The miniature guide to the art of asking essential questions.* Dillon Beach, CA: Foundation for Critical Thinking.

Flaherty, J. (1999). *Coaching: Evoking excellence in others*. Boston: Butterworth-Heinemann.

Goldsmith, M. (1997). Ask, learn, follow-up, and grow. In F. Hesselbein, M. Goldsmith, & R. Beckhard (Eds.), *The Drucker Foundation: The leader of the future* (pp. 227–237). San Francisco: Jossey-Bass.

Hodes, B. (1992). A new foundation in business culture: Managerial coaching. *Industrial Management, 34*(5), 27–28.

Hudson, F. M. (1999). *The handbook of coaching*. San Francisco: Jossey-Bass.

Institute for Professional Empowerment Coaching. (2005). *Coach training manual.* Manalapan, NJ: Author.

Johnson, D. W., & Johnson, R. T. (1995). *Creative controversy: Intellectual challenge in the classroom* (3rd ed.). Edina, MN: Interaction Book Company.

Johnson, D. W., Johnson, R. T., & Smith, K. A. (1997). *Academic controversy: Enriching college instruction through intellectual conflict.* (ERIC Document Reproduction Service No. ED 409 828)

Johnson, K., Sulzer-Azaroff, B., & Mass, C. (1977). The effect of internal proctoring upon examination of performance in a personalized instruction course. *Journal of Personalized Instruction, 1,* 113–117.

Kanter, R. M., & Zolner, J. P. (1986). What the "new" coaches can teach managers. *Management Review, 75*(11), 10–11.

Longenecker, C. O., & Pinkel, G. (1997). Coaching to win at work. *Manage, 48*(2), 19–21.

MacKenzie, A. A., & White, R. T. (1982). Fieldwork in geography and long-term memory. *American Educational Research Journal, 19,* 623–632.

McKeachie, W. J. (1986). *Teaching tips: A guidebook for the beginning college instructor* (3rd ed.). Lexington, MA: D. C. Heath.

McKeachie, W. J., Pintrich, P., Lin, Y., & Smith, D. (1986). *Teaching and learning in the college classroom: A review of the research literature.* Ann Arbor, MI: National Center for Research to Improve Post-Secondary Teaching and Learning, University of Michigan.

Michaels, S., & O'Connor, M. C. (2002). *Accountable talk: Classroom conversation that works* [CD-ROM]. Pittsburgh, PA: University of Pittsburgh.

O'Neil, D. A., & Hopkins, M. M. (2002, August). The "teacher as coach" approach: Pedagogical choices for management educators. *Journal of Management Education, 26*(4), 402–414.

Ruggiero, V. (1988). *Teaching thinking across the curriculum*. New York: Harper & Row.

Semb, G. B., & Ellis, J. A. (1994). Knowledge taught in school: What is remembered? *Review of Educational Research, 64*(2), 253–286.

Silverman, R., Welty, W., & Lyon, S. (1992). *Case studies for teacher problem solving.* New York: McGraw-Hill.

Specht, L. B., & Sandlin, P. K. (1991). The differential effects of experiential learning activities and traditional lecture classes in accounting. *Simulation and Gaming, 22,* 196–210.

Stix, A. (1990). *Creative arts and sciences program* (Vol. 3). New York: Gifted and Talented Enrichment Center.

Stix, A. (1992). *The development and field testing of a multi-modal method for teaching mathematical concepts to preservice teachers by utilizing pictorial journal writing.* Unpublished doctoral dissertation, Columbia University Teachers College, Ann Arbor, MI. (Dissertation Information Service No. 92–18719)

Stix, A. (1993). *Active strategies for interdisciplinary instruction* (Vol. 2). New York: The Interactive Classroom.

Stix, A. (1994). *Teaching strategies for cooperative learning.* New York: The Interactive Classroom.

Stix, A. (1998a). Lobbyist Hearing. *Gems of AGATE, 22*(4), 26–27.

Stix, A. (1998b). Stix Discussion. *Gems of AGATE, 22*(1), 20–21.

Stix, A. (2000). Negotiable contracting. *Gems of AGATE, 24*(3), 20–21.

Stix, A. (2001). *Using literature and simulations in your social studies classroom.* Huntington Beach, CA: Teacher Created Materials.

Stix, A. (2002). Creating rubrics through negotiable contracting. In C. Boston (Ed.), *Understanding scoring rubrics. A guide for teachers* (pp. 66–71). Washington, DC: U.S. Department of Education.

Stix, A. (2004). *Social studies strategies for active learning.* Huntington Beach, CA: Teacher Created Materials.

Stix, A. & Hrbek, F. (2001a). *Exploring History series: The Civil War.* Huntington Beach, CA: Teacher Created Materials.

Stix, A. & Hrbek, F. (2001b). *Exploring History series: The Constitution and a new government.* Huntington Beach, CA: Teacher Created Materials.

Stix, A. & Hrbek, F. (2002a). *Exploring History series: Ancient Greece.* Huntington Beach, CA: Teacher Created Materials.

Stix, A. & Hrbek, F. (2002b). *Exploring History series: Ancient Rome.* Huntington Beach, CA: Teacher Created Materials.

Stix, A. & Hrbek, F. (2002c). *Exploring History series: The Roaring Twenties and the Depressing Thirties.* Huntington Beach, CA: Teacher Created Materials.

Stix, A. & Hrbek, F. (2004). *Exploring History series: The Renaissance.* Huntington Beach, CA: Teacher Created Materials.

Surges, P. T., Ellis, J. A., & Wulfeck, W. H. (1981). *Effects of performance-oriented text upon long-term retention of factual material.* San Diego, CA: Navy Personnel Research and Development Center.

Taba, H. (1971). *Hilda Taba teaching strategies program.* Miami, FL: Institute for Staff Development.

Whitworth, L., Kimsey-Hous, H., & Sandahl, P. (1988). *Co-active coaching.* Palo Alto, CA: Davies-Black.

Index

Note: Information presented in figures is denoted by *f*.

About the Authors

Andi Stix is a national educational consultant, administrator, and certified coach who has been actively teaching for over 30 years. She addresses conferences and conventions across the United States as a keynote speaker or seminar presenter. Stix earned her doctorate from Columbia University and currently owns and operates the Interactive Classroom, an educational consulting firm in New Rochelle, New York. The Interactive Classroom philosophy and activities have been incorporated into the curricula of many school systems throughout the country.

Along with her coauthor, Frank Hrbek, Andi has written a series of simulations and hands-on investigations in history for the secondary school market. The Exploring History series is a three-time winner of New York State's Social Studies Program of Excellence Award, as well as of the Middle States Council for the Social Studies' Social Studies Program of Excellence Certificate. The series also received the Outstanding Curriculum Development Award from the National Association of Gifted Children, and the Teacher Choice Award from *Learning* magazine. For her work in professional development, Andi received the Alexinia Baldwin Educator of the Year Award.

Andi's published articles can be found in *Social Education, Middle School Journal, Social Studies*, and *Gems of AGATE*. She has also authored many books, including *Using Literature and Simulations in Your Social Studies Classroom* (2001), *Integrated Cooperative Strategies for the Social Studies, Language*

Arts, and the Humanities (1997), *Strategies for Student-Centered Assessment* (1996), *Teaching Strategies for Cooperative Learning* (1994), and *Active Strategies for Curriculum Integration* (1993).

Frank Hrbek, coauthor of the Exploring History series, has been a middle school social studies teacher in the New York City school system for close to 40 years. He is a graduate of New York University, where he majored in English with minors in journalism and history. For his master level work, Frank majored in history. In recent years, he has aided Andi Stix in workshops, conferences, and hands-on college-level courses. Frank successfully tested many of Andi's new cooperative learning strategies in his classroom.

Questions, comments, and speaking or workshop inquiries can be directed to Andi Stix at The Interactive Classroom, 27 Siebrecht Place, New Rochelle, New York 10804. She may be reached at 914-636-0888 and astix@optonline.net. Or you may choose to visit her Web sites: www.classroomcoaches.com for educational coaching and workshop training, www.interactiveclassroom.com for interdisciplinary and hands-on learning, www.exploringhistory.com for secondary school social studies curricula, or www.gteckids.com for gifted and talented education.

Related ASCD Resources: Motivating Students

At the time of publication, the following ASCD resources were available; for the most up-to-date information about ASCD resources, go to www.ascd.org. ASCD stock numbers are noted in parentheses.

Books

Accountability for Learning: How Teachers and School Leaders Can Take Charge, by Douglas B. Reeves (#104004)

Activating and Engaging Habits of Mind, by Arthur L. Costa and Bena Kallick (#100033)

The Big Picture: Education Is Everyone's Business, by Dennis Littky and Samantha Grabelle (#104438)

Multimedia

Emotional Intelligence Professional Inquiry Kit, by Pam Robbins and Jane Scott (#997146)

Project-Based Learning with Multimedia (CD ROM), by the San Mateo County Office of Education (#502117)

Video

High Schools at Work: Creating Student-Centered Learning Three Tape Series with Facilitator's Guide (#406117)

Educating Everybody's Children, Tape 4. Increasing Interest, Motivation, and Engagement (#400225)

For more information, visit us on the World Wide Web (http://www. ascd. org), send an e-mail message to member@ascd.org, call the ASCD Service Center (1-800-933-ASCD or 703-578-9600, then press 2), send a fax to 703-575-5400, or write to Information Services, ASCD, 1703 N. Beauregard St., Alexandria, VA 22311-1714 USA.